the

**15-minute
prayer** solution

the
15-minute
prayer solution

HOW **ONE PERCENT** OF YOUR DAY
CAN TRANSFORM YOUR LIFE

gary jansen

LOYOLA PRESS.
A JESUIT MINISTRY
Chicago

LOYOLA PRESS.
A JESUIT MINISTRY

3441 N. Ashland Avenue
Chicago, Illinois 60657
(800) 621-1008
www.loyolapress.com

Previously published in a different version as *Exercising Your Soul*, Hachette, 2010

Scripture quotations contained herein are from the *New Revised Standard Version Bible: Catholic Edition*, copyright © 1993 and 1989 by the Division of Christian Education of the National Council of the Churches of Christ in the U.S.A. Used by permission. All rights reserved.

Cover art credit: © iStock/Hong Li

ISBN-13: 978-0-8294-4407-0
ISBN-10: 0-8294-4407-6
Library of Congress Control Number: 2015951189

Printed in the United States of America.

18 19 20 21 22 23 24 25 26 27 Versa 10 9 8 7 6 5 4 3 2

For Grace,

Eddie, and Charlie,

the joys of my life.

Contents

Pray constantly.
—St. Paul, from his First Letter to
the Thessalonians, 5:17

Don't be an idiot.
—Judge Judy

Part One: The Reason Why

The old man and the boy were walking through a park.

"See those two trees over there?" said the old man.

"Yes," said the boy.

"See the distance between them? See how their branches almost touch each other? *Almost*, but never do?"

"Yes."

"The tree on the left *adores* the tree on the right. And I'm pretty sure the tree on the right feels the same way about the tree on the left. They can't stop looking at each other. Did you hear what I said?"

The boy, startled, answered, "Yes."

The old man sighed. "No matter how much they yearn to be closer to each other they can never touch. They can never touch each other's happiness. They can never touch each other's suffering. If one gets sick, the other one can only watch, can't help. They are locked apart from each other forever."

"Unless lightning knocks one of them over onto the other," said the boy.

"Yes, you're right," said the old man. They stood together silently for a while, the wind blowing the branches of the trees. The old man smiled.

The boy looked up. "This makes me sad and angry," he said. "What are you smiling about?"

"Don't be sad," said the old man. "Yes, the branches of the trees can never touch. They can never hug. But if you go below the surface, the roots of these two very separate trees are entwined and entangled. What they yearn for above, they experience deep below. We can't see it, but they share one life. What happens to one, happens to the other."

The boy thought for a moment, nodded, and said, "I'm hungry."

"Me too. Let's go."

1

White Rabbits

Did you know that there are 1,440 minutes in a day? It's true. I did the math. Did you also know that one percent of all that time is fourteen minutes and twenty-four seconds? What would happen if you made a conscious decision, every day, to exercise your soul by giving roughly fifteen minutes of your time over to God? Just one tiny percent of your life. Would your life change?

Mine did.

The book you have in your hands is a result of that spiritual experiment. This book is not a memoir (though I do share a number of personal stories with you in the pages that follow); it is *essentially* a book on prayer. Not the namby-pamby, rattling-off-a-wish-list, "Oh, please let me have nice things" kind of prayer. (Who am I kidding—just five minutes ago I asked to win the lottery . . . again!) I'm talking about simple, *effective* prayer, the type that does not have to take a lot of time and will ultimately help you answer life's most daunting questions (Why am I here? What difference does my life make? Do I *really* want fries with that?), leading you on a path to experiencing God more boldly, deeply, and intimately. And let's face it, in our fast-paced, overextended, attention-deficit, twittering world, whether you're a student, a busy mom, a stressed-out father, a single woman struggling to find a job, a guy looking for a girlfriend, a loner, a freak, a geek, or the life-of-the-party with all the friends in the world, prayer needs to be effective to be worth our time (and God's time too). Otherwise, why do it?

This collection of reflections, anecdotes, stories, and exercises—the result of that one percent change in my life and inspired in many ways by the spirituality of St. Ignatius, a sixteenth-century Spanish soldier and mystic with a strong Protestant work ethic (even though he was Catholic) and a unique way of relating to God (more on that in the pages that follow)—may appear to be masquerading as a self-help book. I can assure you it is no such thing. As an editor who has worked in publishing for many years, I have read and edited my share of self-help books. Many of them are terrific, informative, and, well, very helpful. Almost all of them, however, put the self first, meaning you (or if not you, the author). Not a bad thing for the genre, but we who are believers should put nothing before God.

The Fifteen-Minute Prayer Solution, then, is a *God-help* book, not because I think the world revolves around me, but because all life, all people, all things—all assistance—come from God.

Much talk is made of the idea of grace, God's unmerited gift of love to us, as if God created some people to receive this blessing and others not. For all I know, this may be true—maybe God does play favorites—but I don't believe this. All of creation is ever present in God. You. Me. That annoying person at your job. That waffle you ate this morning. The coffee cup you just threw away. *Everything.*

Many of us may already think this, but the trick is not just perceiving grace in the brain, but *feeling* it in the heart. *It's about having the experience.*

If you have ever shared an intimate part of yourself with a beloved so that that person can experience something you cherish, then you can understand why I wrote this book. I am not a theologian, nor am I a mystic or an intellectual. I am a beggar and have been knocking outside God's door for some time now. Sometimes I knock and there's no answer. But I'm a stubborn kind of fellow with my mind made up on God, so I just keep knocking. Eventually, the door opens and I'm given some bread, an experience of God that satisfies this deep hunger I have inside. But I must admit, I'm ravenous and I always desire more. Even though I'm still hungry I want to share some of this bread with you. Just a tiny crumb of it can transform your life.

I mentioned St. Ignatius, and many have summed up his spirituality as a way of finding God in all things. We can find God in our friends and family (and even our enemies). We can find God in nature or the pages of a great book or projected back to us from a TV or computer screen. Yet finding God in all things is the end result. We have to do something before that. We need to seek him out! Is he hiding under a basket? Is he somewhere in that tall tree? Is he staring back at me from the eyes of someone sprawled out on a city street? Is he speaking to me through my wife and sons? (Yes. Yes. Yes. Yes!) So before we can find God, we need to *seek God everywhere*. Yet seeking God everywhere can be daunting. You need to build your spiritual muscles to be up to the task. There can be a lot of disappointment along the way, a number of detours, dead ends (though as we'll see later we can seek God there too). All this is why some years ago I made a commitment to dedicate at least fifteen minutes, one percent of my day, to daily prayer and meditation, two things that can be mind-blowingly exciting or downright, drudgingly boring!

Still, if you want to get anywhere in life, whether in school or at a job, you have to be consistent and you need to be open to change. Sometimes something won't be working for you in a class or with your boss. If you keep doing that ineffective thing over and over again, it will ultimately lead to a form of disappointment or disaster. Show up to your job consistently late and you'll get fired. Then again, realizing that it might be better to show up to your class early every day (after being reprimanded by your teacher a number of times) to study a few minutes before everyone shows up, well, you have a decent shot at excelling at what you're doing. "Slow and steady wins the race," some say. Not me. Slow and steady means you'll finish the race, but a marathon might take a week to complete at that pace. Instead, I prefer, "Hard work *and* steady wins the race," not just in the workplace, at home, or at school, but in your spirituality as well. At the same time, you don't want to exhaust yourself. I know this from experience. Bear with me: here's a little backstory.

From a very early age I had a deep desire to know God. Looking back on my life, I don't think this is surprising. I grew up in the shadow of a great twentieth-century cathedral, St. Agnes, by far one of the tallest structures on Long Island. I attended Catholic school for twelve years. And my mother was a bit of a suburban mystic, a woman who decorated our home with various images of Jesus Christ and the Virgin Mary, bought us rosary beads for our birthdays, and talked of visions and saints and holy ghosts.

There was *God talk* all around me—at home, at school, at church, and even in dreams. (I remember one recurring dream I had as a teenager when I asked Jesus what the meaning of life was. He never told me . . . until years later.) Still, for whatever reason, I just didn't *feel* a connection to God, who was supposedly so important in our lives. In some ways, he was like an uncle I never met—the one in Canada with a drinking problem.

Everyone else seemed to know God. He was well liked. There were always stories to be told and photos around the house reminding me that he existed ("Look, here he is at a wedding with a glass of wine in his hand" or "This is a shot of him with all those children on his lap"), but I had absolutely no emotional connection to him.

God, who seemed so present for my mother, my grandmother, and my teachers, was elusive to me. God was like a white rabbit. Not the white rabbit that Grace Slick and the Jefferson Airplane sang about back in the sixties. Nor do I mean the white rabbit from *Alice in Wonderland* (though we will see that living a spiritual life is a lot like falling into a certain kind of Wonderland). I mean the white rabbit I saw in the woods one day when I was twelve years old.

While I was growing up, my family lived less than a mile from Hempstead Lake, one of only a few freshwater lakes on Long Island. When I was old enough to go off on my own, I would invariably ride my bike across town and go exploring in the woods around the lake. I don't know why, maybe it was an infatuation with King Arthur or the *Lord of the Rings*, but I always felt that I was going to hear a voice coming out of the lake or I would find a magic ring and take flight on a giant bubble to a faraway land. I enjoyed exploring, most of all during the autumn months, when the land around the lake looked like daytime fireworks—explosions of red, yellow, and orange.

It was during one of these days wandering around alone in the woods that I saw something white flash in front of me. I stopped, frightened. Thinking about it now, I can still feel my heart pulsating in my left ear the way I did that day. I tried listening past my fear and heard crunching. It sounded like some kind of giant. I was old enough to be out by myself but not old enough not to believe in monsters. I took a few steps to my right and soon had a clear view of the monstrosity!

A little white rabbit, his ears high, his nose twitching. He was munching on some kind of leaf. He was definitely not what I would call a giant.

I don't know what came over me, because instantly I turned into some kind of gunless Elmer Fudd. I had one thought in my head: *I'm gonna catch this wascally wabbit!* I took a few steps toward the tiny scoundrel and we locked eyes. I took another step. The rabbit's shoulders seemed to be growing right in front of me. I was midway through my next step when the rabbit darted faster than anything I have ever seen in my life. I ran after it, over fallen branches and layers of dry leaves. I don't remember how far I ran, just that I quickly became winded and stopped. I remember bending over, my hands on my knees, panting and looking up and seeing the rabbit, still some distance away, staring back at me.

I took a deep breath. "I'm going to get you now," I said—and ran. The rabbit again took flight and darted deeper into the woods. I ran maybe another fifty feet and stopped. This happened again and again, and the deeper I went into the big woods, the more afraid I became that I would never find my way out (walking through those woods now, I see I was never really more than a couple of hundred feet from a road, but at the time it seemed like an endless vale). At a certain point I gave up, and even though at the time there was nothing I desired more, I let the rabbit go. I looked around and slowly made my way back to a path that eventually led me back to the lake.

I have never forgotten that day in the woods, and over the years I've come to see that moment as a metaphor for my spiritual life. God was, in many ways, like that white rabbit. There was this mysterious, beautiful creature I wanted to capture and hold. I would run after God with all my might, only to become winded and discouraged when he would move away from me. No matter how hard I tried, God was always out of reach. I became convinced that God never wanted me to catch up. This was how I viewed the Almighty for most of my life: a quick-footed rabbit, a trickster—Bugs Bunny, only not as funny.

Then, a few years ago, I began to pray. I mean *really pray*. Not the halfhearted, going-through-the-motions kind of praying we do at church ("Dear God, you're great, but I'd rather be home sleeping"). Not the jabbering, making-deals-with-the-Almighty kind of praying ("Look, I know I'm not the most patient person in the world, but I promise to be really good if you let me kiss Mona Kenny, just once"), but serious, formal prayer, something I had never tried.

While I was growing up, prayer bored me, but now that I could actually grow a beard (some could debate this), the more I did it, the more it excited me. I soon began to realize that even though I was raised in a religious household and spent over a decade in Catholic schools, I was prayer illiterate.

Within a short time, by praying just a few minutes every day, my life began to change, and soon the rabbit in those autumnal woods began to slow down. I was getting a much better look at him. He was still mysterious, but now when I would set off in pursuit, the white rabbit that haunted my waking and sleeping moments for over ten years seemed willing to let me follow him. As I moved toward him, he would wait, and as I reached him, the rabbit would again scamper off, but only a few feet. He would turn, stand, and face me, and I would follow. The rabbit wasn't running away from me. He was leading me to another place. It was soon thereafter that I realized God hadn't slowed down, *I had slowed down . . .* I had stopped running and that made all the difference.

Everything came alive for me. Things I had never noticed before began to take shape. I could now see the path I was on, I could taste the trees around me in my heart, I could hear a world I'd never heard before. I could feel the air on my neck, and for the first time in my life, I glimpsed the eyes of God.

I had been transformed.

What I realize now was that I had been suffering from a form of spiritual anorexia. Even though I had grown up with religion all around me—and it was just about everywhere I went—I hadn't let it enter into me. God, it now seemed, had been a banquet, but I had been a spoiled child who refused to eat. Something was keeping me away from nourishing my soul and in turn nourishing a relationship with God. My soul was hungry but I had never opened my mouth.

Prayer soon led me to meditation, and meditation soon led me back to prayer, so that the two became entwined in my life in a way I never knew was possible. The more I spent time with God, the more I felt myself becoming stronger in my day-to-day life. This is not to say I wasn't weak—I had been asleep for over twenty years of my life. And though any kind of spiritual muscle had atrophied to a point of almost becoming vestigial, with each minute I spent in prayer, I felt myself coming back to life. The scary thing is, for most of my life, I didn't even know I was dead.

After a few months of doing what I was calling "my daily one percent spiritual regimen" (prayer) followed by meditation, followed by prayer, followed by meditation—my vision started to change. By this, I don't mean I needed new glasses, but in many ways it was a bit like going to the eye doctor.

When you have your eyes examined, the optometrist will put your head in a strange contraption, place lenses before your eyes, and ask you to read the letters you see on the wall across from you. She will then change the focus of the lens and ask you if the image is better or worse. Depending on how you answer, she will change the focus again and again until you realize that the initial image, which seemed clear, was in fact quite blurry. You had grown so used to living in an unfocused world that you didn't know better.

That's how I felt. I had been blind but now I could see—not fully, I was still legally spiritually blind—but I could see glimpses, colors, and textures I had never seen before, and it scared me.

In the weeks and months that followed, everywhere I looked I saw emaciated souls: in my friends, in my family, in my coworkers, and in the people on the street. On the surface most of these people were beautiful and smart and funny, but their spirits seemed unhealthy and in definite need of nourishment. This is not to say I considered myself anything special, but seeing them helped me realize why so many people who seem to have so much going for them experience disillusionment and loneliness.

Every year millions of people spend thousands of dollars nurturing their bodies, exercising their muscles, supplementing their diets with vitamins and wonder drugs. Millions more people spend even more money exercising their minds by attending school in one form or another. Yet how many of those people spend a fraction of that time or money on exercising their souls every day? Certainly, some people do; the whole New Age mind, body, spirit industry wouldn't exist if some people weren't out there doing yoga and meditating. But many Catholics and Christians, even the churchgoing ones, are still catching up to the idea that prayer and meditation should be—and need to be—a daily activity.

Most doctors recommend that you work out at least three days a week. Most students attend class at least five days a week. Yet many of us may attend a religious service once a week and think, *Well, that's done.* But that's not enough. Your cardiologist wouldn't say, "Hey Bill, look, I want you to run forty-five minutes on Sunday and then take the rest of the week off," would he?

Imagine this story: Once upon a time there was a young man who smoked a cigarette. It made him cough and choke, but something about it made him feel good too. So he smoked another. He didn't cough as much this time. So he decided to try it a third time.

"Well, that was nice," he said. "I was feeling anxious before, but now I feel calm." He smoked some more, and within a year he was up to three packs a day.

Ten years later the man went to his doctor for a checkup.

"Phil, you need to stop smoking."

"Why?"

"Because if you don't, you're going to die."

"Are you sure?"

"Phil, how many packs do you smoke a day?"

"Three."

Phil's doctor took out a prescription pad and started doing math: sixty cigarettes multiplied by 365 days multiplied by ten years. Phil, it seemed, had smoked 219,000 cigarettes in ten years' time. Over two hundred thousand cigarettes.

"You put smoke in your lungs almost a quarter of a million times, Phil."

Phil quit soon thereafter.

Most of us would agree that smoking is a bad habit. I think we can all agree that the physical size of a cigarette isn't that big, is it? It weighs very little and really, how long does one cigarette last? Five minutes? If you smoke two hundred thousand cigarettes in ten years and each cigarette lasts five minutes, then you've spent over one million minutes of your life smoking. That's over sixteen thousand hours, nearly two full years of your life smoking cigarettes.

Many of us excel at cultivating bad habits, but what about a good habit? What about incorporating into our lives daily prayer and meditation? What if instead of smoking a cigarette, you "smoked" a prayer or some form of spiritual exercise sixty times a day? That would mean smoking God for three hundred minutes a day. What would that do to the state of your soul? Don't be frightened. This book isn't about giving five hours to God, just fifteen tiny minutes. But from small things, big things do come.

So let's get started. If a journey of a thousand miles begins with a single step, then I hope this book will serve as a pair of good walking shoes you put on before your feet even touch the ground. And if you are somewhere out there along the road already, in a town you've never heard of, standing outside an all-night diner, staring up at a black sky dotted with stars, I pray this book can be a touch of light reading that brings comfort between your arrivals and departures.

2

What Is a Spiritual Exercise?

A spiritual exercise is any practice that draws you closer to an experience of union with the divine. These practices can take the form of various types of prayer, meditation, or contemplation—three separate and distinct actions that are too often considered interchangeable.

In many ways spiritual exercises are like courting a beloved. You have this desire, this yearning for another, and you suffer this gravitational pull to *do something*: touch, smell, listen, taste, to look upon this person who seems to be calling you from a place other than this strange, fragmented world we live in. When you and your beloved can't be together, for all the reasons that seem to keep lovers apart—distance, time, family, work—you spend your moments daydreaming, fantasizing, worshiping, writing love letters, seeking out gifts, scheduling times to meet alone, all in the hopes of surrendering—of collapsing like a star—in utter rapture with the other.

Yes, doing a spiritual exercise is like going on a date with God.

While spiritual exercises are common in many religions, many people associate the term with *The Spiritual Exercises of Ignatius of Loyola*, a sort of military manual for the human soul, written by the Spanish priest who founded the Jesuit order in 1540. Ignatius, a former knight injured by a cannonball while defending Pamplona from the French, had a spiritual awakening shortly thereafter and pursued a course of spiritual exploration that led to his writing, which in turn transformed the way many of us approach a relationship with the Almighty.

Anyone who has tried to read through the *Spiritual Exercises*, though, knows it can be a daunting task, albeit an important and gratifying one. The information contained within that text can open windows to the soul that allow the warm, windy breath of the Holy Spirit to clear out spiritual rooms that reek of mothballs and stale experience.

Essentially, the Exercises can lead to a greater awareness of the eternally alive God in the temporal experiences of our daily lives. Few books rival it in terms of importance in

Christian spirituality. Yet the language Ignatius uses is dense and the practices are sometimes overly strenuous for the average person. Ignatius's *Spiritual Exercises* is sort of like James Joyce's *Ulysses*: a book many people talk about but few people have read from cover to cover.

But what if you're a mom with very little time on your hands or a father working two jobs to support your family, and you have this burning desire to know God but very little time or patience to read through a sixteenth-century work written for members of a religious order?

In this book, I have loosely borrowed the idea of spiritual exercises from Ignatius and have incorporated some of his basic ideas—the importance of the imagination in prayer, meditation, and the reading of Scripture—into a book for the twenty-first-century reader.

That's right, for people with very little time on their hands.

Don't be fooled into thinking that simple things can't be, at the same time, difficult and complex. As Brother Lawrence, a French monk who lived nearly a hundred years after Ignatius, wrote in *Practicing the Presence of God*:

> We must be careful not to be deceived into thinking that this union is a simple expression of the heart, as in saying, "My God, I love You with all my heart," or other similar words. No, this union is something indefinable that is found in a gentle, peaceable, spiritual, reverent, humble,

loving, and utterly simple soul. This "indefinable something" raises the soul and presses it to love God, to worship Him and yes, even to caress Him with an inexpressible tenderness known only to those who experience it.

We as human beings are attracted to the unknown. Many of us fall in love less with the known aspects of an individual than with the mystery that lies beyond the seen. Yes, on the surface I can fall in love with a smile or a laugh, but those things are just signposts to something else: a fiery desire to hear an orchestra of angels in the eyes of a beloved, to see the colors of music in a long-awaited, hoped-for arrival, to taste the tongue of the divine in the whispered embrace of a departure.

It is in this unknown that we find a connection that binds us to God and to one another. This connection is none other than Holy Spirit. Some things exist beyond ourselves. God, however, is not one of them. Some of us may accept this intellectually—that the Spirit of God lives in each and every one of us—but it is the objective of this book to move away from the mind, to stop thinking, and to descend not into nothingness, but to the depths of *everythingness*, a place where every thing, every person, every moment, every desire, every yearning is connected—and all those things are connected to God. It is a place of perpetual prayer, a place where you no longer *practice* the presence of God; you *experience* that presence fully in body and soul—two components of our existence that are intricately woven together.

This is the heart of the spiritual life.

When many of us talk about spiritual matters, there tends to be an "easier said than done" sword of Damocles stationed above our heads that keeps us from taking the step forward: *Oh, I'd like to spend more time with God, but I'm just too busy. Oh, I just can't sit still for that long. Oh, it's boring. Oh, I tried and it was just too difficult for me. Oh, what good is prayer going to do anyway?*

Living a spiritual life is not difficult. Certainly *it can be*, the way walking from a living room to a kitchen can be difficult if I decided to throw my legs in the air and walk on my hands. I, like you, am created in God's image, but I am no acrobat. I would certainly fall on my tailbone and do some serious damage to my body.

Living a spiritual or prayerful life can be as simple as drinking a glass of water. If you are blessed to have a relatively sound body and mind, and equally blessed to live in a home with clean running water, it's really as easy as *realizing* you're thirsty, deciding to take action, and then standing up from your chair, walking to the kitchen, taking a glass off your shelf, turning on the faucet, and drinking. *Ah, refreshing. I didn't realize I was that thirsty. Let me have another.*

The spiritual life can be that way too. I felt thirsty. I decided I needed some water. I took a drink. Wow, was I actually starting to turn to sand? I had no idea.

This doesn't mean that leading a spiritual life does not require effort on our parts, but I can assure you, as someone who has grown into a spiritual life—not through my own efforts but through God's, who wills this for all people—a little goes a very long way. In many instances, all it takes are small changes in your life. A single prayer has more power than you ever thought possible.

This also does not mean that, once you embark on a spiritual life, you won't encounter difficulty. Spiritual living doesn't make you immune to life's troubles, but it does give you strength. With the power of the Holy Spirit, these exercises, like physical exercises, will make you stronger. Allow me to demonstrate how.

Imagine for a moment that there are two people standing on a tree branch ten feet above the ground. Both people are of equal height and weight. Yet one person is physically fit and the other person is out of shape. They have the same body mass, only one has muscle and the other person has flab. Do you have that picture in your mind?

Now, kick them both off the tree branch at the same time, using equal force in your kick. Both victims, in our little imagining, hit the ground at the same time. Gravity, it seems, does not play favorites.

Which one suffers fewer injuries?

The answer?

Well, it's a trick question. They both suffer sprained ankles. *But which one recovers faster?*

Well, the person who was physically fit, that's who. Our imagined out-of-shape person ends up suffering pain in his tendon for the rest of his days.

The same is true of the spiritual life. All of us will experience moments of joy and sorrow, ease and struggle, loneliness and elation, whether it be at the birth or death of a loved one, a new job that turns out not to be what was expected, disappointments in friendships, financial insecurities, or the devastations caused by war. Difficulties do not go away when one undertakes the spiritual journey.

In fact, the road to spiritual fitness can be wild and overrun by brush and thorns. There is the likelihood of getting cut. In most cases, leading a spiritual life means struggle, because as you begin to turn your focus more and more to God, the more you realize that the life you were living wasn't much of a life at all. Yet if your soul is fit, you will have the strength to face these challenges in a courageous way, and, if injuries do occur while you are walking—and sometimes running—on this path, you'll be able to recover faster and not be deterred from your goal, which is union with God.

Far too many of us approach the spiritual life "with too little patience," Pope John Paul II wrote in his book *The Way to Christ*, "as if it were a matter of something like a surgical operation or an injection, which will immediately make us better again. Change is a long-term process."

What frightens people away from a fitness plan, whether it's physical or spiritual, is fear of the short-term negative impact on their lives. I am a firm believer that people are not afraid of change itself. If I said to you, "I'm going to transform your life by giving you a million dollars," would you fear that? You might be afraid I had recently escaped from Bellevue, or that the money I have to give you was stolen from a Wall Street robber baron. But if everything was legitimate, you'd do cartwheels.

On the other hand, if I said to you, "I'm going to install a new complicated computer system at your job that's going to make your life difficult and will take you twice as long to do your work," you're going to start shaking. People don't fear change. They fear that their lives are going to be worse off than they were before the change. Change, in many ways, needs to happen by the spoonful.

One last reason people seem to stay away from leading a spiritual life is tiredness. We may be tired of our families, our friends, our jobs. We may be tired of waiting at the same red light every day on the way to school. We may be tired of our neighbors. We may be tired of crime in our neighborhoods or of never catching a break. We may be tired because no matter how hard we try we can't save any money. We may be tired of the same old news we hear every day: the world is at war, terrorism is on the rise, murder is happening everywhere, the economy is failing, our leaders are idiots, and the movie star we admire so much is a bad tipper.

We may be tired because no matter how hard we try, we can't lose weight. We may be tired because of an illness. Tired because someone we love is spiraling out of control because of an addiction. We may be tired of our children not listening to us. We may be tired of feeling isolated, of feeling alone, or feeling weak. Tired of being frustrated, disappointed, moody, irritable, broken. We may be tired that no matter how hard we pray, we never hear God speaking to us.

Tiredness is one of the biggest culprits keeping people away from the spiritual life. Prayer and meditation are surefire ways to energize you. They're even better than Red Bull and Pop Rocks. And while many people believe that what they are looking for in their lives is rest—St. Augustine's often-quoted "We are restless, Lord, until we find rest in you" comes to mind—when we turn our lives toward God, rest is the very last thing we could want. And if you don't believe me, what happens every time the Holy Spirit makes an appearance in the New Testament?

Someone takes action.

We are at rest, Lord, until we wake up and take action in you.

Ultimately, to live a spiritual life, all it takes is a slight shift of our focus. Certainly the *Titanic* could have been saved from disaster if it had shifted its direction when leaving port by a single degree south. A single degree.

What changes would happen in our lives if we shifted our focus by a single degree? What would happen to us if we made just a tiny little change and gave just fifteen minutes daily to exercising our souls by giving that time to God? That's just one percent; the other ninety-nine percent you can do whatever you want with. Want to find out?

Come. It is time for you to step forward and redefine what it means to be human in the eyes of God, by seeing God in all things. It's time to strengthen that soul of yours.

Wait. What is a soul? Good question.

3

Souls, Mustard Seeds, and Redefining Humanity

According to the theologian John A. Hardon, a soul is "the spiritual immortal part in human beings that animates their bodies."

Awesome!

But what does that mean?

Keeping that definition in mind, please consider that the soul isn't some dry intellectual concept, but a vibrant, energizing, electrifying component of our lives. The soul is not complete in itself—it needs to give life to a body. It is, however, the part of us that gives our existence meaning.

The soul is, in many ways, like an electric frying pan. It's connected to an energy source. Sometimes the pan is cold, warm, or hot. It takes the individual ingredients of our lives—our joys, sorrows, disappointments, and questions;

the people, places, things; our relationships; our bodies, sensations, and emotions—and cooks them. It brings all these pieces of our lives together. Salt is added and everything coalesces into something new. No longer do we have a bunch of heated, separate ingredients; we have a meal.

What does a meal do? It nourishes us. It gives us strength. It transforms us. It brings people together. It satisfies a hunger.

In this analogy, God is our source, the heat is the living Holy Spirit, Jesus is the salt that brings out our essence (for those who can't have sodium, Jesus is like Mrs. Dash), and through the gift of free will, we control the degree to which our lives, our meals, are formed. The trick, as in all cooking, is knowing what the right temperature should be. Cook your food at too low a temperature and you end up waiting years for it to be ready. By that time, everyone either has ordered takeout or has gone to sleep. Cook your food too high and you risk burning it and a visit from your local firefighters, who aren't going to be too happy when they see that the purported four-alarm was really some burnt turkey-and-bean chili.

Balance, it seems, is key. Many of us know this. As with Icarus, flying too high and too close to the sun means you will burn and crash; fly too low near the water and your wings are weighed down, so you'll drown. Yet in our attempt to find a middle ground, we resign ourselves to living lukewarm lives.

We don't sin in major ways, and we don't do good in major ways either.

In Dante's *Inferno*, lukewarm souls, those who lived without any type of passion or commitment, are some of the most wretched of the damned, and in the New Testament, the lukewarm are spit out of God's mouth. I am absolutely not advocating sin, but there is a certain boldness—granted, a misdirected boldness—in the actions of all great sinners. The problem seems to be an ultimate faith in oneself, a person who dares to act above universal law—God's law. The error isn't in the actual boldness but in the focus. Instead of acting boldly in the name of the Father, we act boldly in the names of ourselves. The error, again, lies in where we shift our attention.

What is hate except a shifting of our focus away from love? What is despair but shifting our focus away from hope? What is anger except a shifting away from forgiveness? And what are we when we shift our attention away from God?

Too many of us who try to lead good lives end up playing it safe. We shift our focus to our own abilities to keep us secure. And if you're playing it safe, how much faith in God do you really have?

We are not called to be sinners. Nor are we called to be lukewarm. We are called by God to be bold, courageous human beings infused with the Holy Spirit. We are called to be heroic. We are called to be miracle workers: "Very truly, I tell you, the one who believes in me will also do the works that I do and, in fact, will do *greater works* than these" (John 14:12, emphasis added).

Human history has, in some ways, helped us forget our own humanity, covering us under thousands of years of fighting, wars, and bloodshed. It is like a jewel encased in mud; there is something precious there, but we just can't see it. Spiritual exercises—daily, directed prayer and meditation—strengthen our faith, and that increased power of belief, in turn, helps us see the beauty under all the coverings.

You may be thinking, *How could something as small as a prayer do all that?* If I were a well-seasoned jazz musician, I'd reply, "It's all about mustard seeds, baby." Since I'm a suburban mall rat, I'll just drop the "baby" and say, "It's all about mustard seeds":

> The kingdom of heaven is like a mustard seed that someone took and sowed in his field; it is the smallest of all the seeds, but when it has grown it is the greatest of shrubs and becomes a tree, so that the birds of the air come and make nests in its branches. (Matthew 13:31–32)

> For truly I tell you, if you have faith the size of a mustard seed, you will say to this mountain, "Move from here to there," and it will move; and nothing will be impossible for you. (Matthew 17:20)

I remember the first time I heard the parable of the mustard seed. It was around the time of my first communion. My teacher at the time was a feisty old crow who cared less for the state of our souls and more about the state of our fingernails. She had some obsession with checking our fingernails for dirt. Every day we all had to walk up to her desk and show our hands. She would check for clean hands and then raise our fingers to her bifocaled eyes and examine under our nails.

Maybe she was a frustrated forensic scientist, I don't know. But if the cleanliness of my hands was any indication of the cleanliness of my soul, well, mine was tainted black and muddy (I liked to play in the dirt a lot then . . . still do). I thought she was the nastiest woman I had ever met, and I think the feeling was mutual—every day I would get hollered at for not having clean hands. I do remember scrubbing them and then washing them daily before I went to school, but somewhere along the way they'd get all dirty again.

Anyway, after one particular examination, she screamed at me, "If you only gave a mustard seed's amount of effort toward washing your hands, you'd have the cleanest hands in the world!"

"What's a mustard seed?" I asked. I knew mustard was something for hot dogs, but I never knew there was a seed.

Other children in the classroom chimed in: "What is a mustard seed?"

She then told us all to get into a circle, and she told us a story. As much as she was a clean-hand militant, Ms. Snyder was a pretty good storyteller. She told us Jesus' parable, and when it was over, the words "If you have the faith of a mustard seed, you can move mountains" circled inside my head.

"I can move mountains?" I asked her.

"Not you. You can't even keep your hands clean."

I felt as if I was going to cry, and I think she felt bad because she changed her tone. "Well, maybe you can, when you get older . . . if you have enough faith."

This was amazing! I was a big-time reader of comic books, and I had asked my parents for years whether people could really fly, if they had superhuman strength and could pick up buildings, if they could use a power ring and create anything that was in their minds, if they had super speed. The answer was always no, but here was my teacher, my fingernail drill sergeant, telling me that one day I might be able to move mountains.

So, I started training. I was going to move mountains.

Well, my first attempt at moving a mountain came during church one day when I tried moving a statue with my mind. I remember focusing on the statue and repeating to myself, *I have faith, now move. I have faith, now move.* I looked up and, well, nothing happened. This did not deter me. *Obviously, I need more training.* Even though a mustard seed seemed awfully small to me, I knew deep down I wasn't the best kid in the world. I was always getting into trouble at home and in school, and my hands—well, I just couldn't get over the whole washing thing, but still I dreamt of moving mountains.

This went on for years. Sometimes I would forget about the story, and other times I would go on these so-called training binges where I would focus on something and try to make it move. I may not have liked Ms. Snyder, but I thought she was always honest with me. In the quiet of my room, I would sit and pray and usually fall asleep. I tried levitating myself once and fell down a flight of stairs.

Well, some years back I found myself in Denver for a conference I had to attend. My faith had waxed and waned over the years, but I was feeling pretty strong spiritually, and since this was the first time I was going to see a tried-and-true mountain, I was going to put my faith to use.

So I rented a car and within five minutes drove into the mountains, which in Denver means driving a block or two, and I pulled over at the side of the road and stood there, looking at a grand, snowcapped mountain Goliath.

"Today, you meet your match, O Large One." (Even as I got older, I spoke in comic-book language.) "It is I, David." (I didn't speak my real name out loud because I didn't want to get in trouble in case I started an earthquake.) "My slingshot is my faith. You will move, mountain."

By this time in my life, my early twenties, I felt pretty confident. I was convinced that I had faith at least the size of a baseball. Okay, maybe a golf ball, but it was definitely bigger than a mustard seed.

"Move, mountain, move," I said.

Nothing.

I closed my eyes.

"Move, mountain, move! Move, mountain, move!"

I kept repeating the phrase for at least five minutes and, well, *I started to feel something.* I started to feel something well up inside me, and I could feel my feet start to tingle.

"Move, mountain, move!"

Each time I said those words, I felt stronger and stronger. I felt as if I were just about to strike oil, that I had my feet planted firmly in the ground and I was drilling into the tectonic plates and I was going to move this mountain. I was convinced! My faith was unstoppable.

I repeated the words one more time: "Move, mountain, move!" I opened my eyes!

Nothing happened.

I think, but I'm not one hundred percent sure, that a bird crapped on my shoulder. Stupid bird.

I stared up at that mountain and that mountain stared back at me. "Mustard seed," it seemed to say to me. "Yeah, sure. Go home, kid."

Well, this crushed me, and I have to admit my faith was shaken by this incident. I didn't stop believing in God, but I started putting limits on what I believed. The parables, for instance, stopped being living truths for me; they became nice stories. They expressed interesting ideas, but they were just that—ideas, fairy tales even—nothing else.

Well, ten years passed, and my spiritual journey took many twists and turns, and I must have come back to that parable I loved so much when I was younger, because one morning I woke from sleep and realized that the story was true! It was true! I was like Ebenezer Scrooge on Christmas morning. Sometime overnight I had had an awakening, and the story was true! And it had been proven in the twentieth century!

It wasn't a priest or a pope or a mystic or Mother Teresa who proved that the story of the mustard seed was legitimate. It was scientists. Einstein. Fermi. Oppenheimer. Atomic physicists! These people believed in something the size of a mustard seed. Actually, they believed in something smaller than a mustard seed, something they couldn't even see—the atom.

These scientists were able to harness the power of the atom. They were able to take something so infinitesimally small and unleash its energy. In the process they created something more powerful than anything human beings had ever created.

The atom bomb.

From one atom, something smaller than a mustard seed, scientists now had enough power to seismically move a mountain. Not only could they shake a mountain, they could destroy one.

Now if you and I are made up of a billion tiny atoms, how much God-given potential—how much God-given power—lies inside each and every one of us? Not to destroy. Not to annihilate mountains, but to move the things in our lives that block us from being truly human and to raise, through the power of Holy Spirit and the grace of God, ourselves and others to new life in union with God.

How do we do this? Well, we can't. God does it through us, but prayer and meditation allow us to knock on God's door so he can answer and allow the gift of human potential—the gift of first life he bestowed on Adam—to flow through us.

We were not created to be flawed creatures. We were called by God to greatness. As much as I love my Christian and

Catholic faith, we believers, as a group, have spent too much time focusing on how vile human beings are. We need to shift that focus. I'm not saying to ignore sin, but when we focus on something, we become that thing. If I focus in my mind on the idea that I'm a loser, I will become a loser. If I focus on becoming a great student, I will become a great student.

Yet somehow we believe that two thousand years of focusing on sin will make us not sin. Hmmm. Who was the marketing genius that came up with that one? The devil's greatest power isn't possessing someone's soul; it's distraction.

In 1843, Nathaniel Hawthorne, the author of *The Scarlet Letter*, published a short story called "The Birthmark." At the center of this tale is a beautiful young woman with a tiny hand-shaped birthmark on her face. She is the talk of the town, praised for her beauty and desired by many. There is one young man, a scientist, who falls for the gorgeous young woman, courts her, and eventually marries her. After their wedding, the young man becomes obsessed with his wife's birthmark, and as the days wear on, he begins to see her as ugly, as a perfect being marred by this hideous defect. Soon the young woman buys into her husband's opinion and considers herself an abomination.

The young scientist decides he can create a way to get rid of the mark and make this near-perfect creature perfect. He gives her a potion to drink. She drinks, and the mark fades. The young man has gained what he has always wanted: perfection.

Minutes later his wife dies, and his moment of perfection, the love of his life, is lost forever.

Each of us has a birthmark. This mark is very real and can be quite dangerous, but over the last two thousand years we have focused less on the beauty of the creation and more on the defect. How many of us grew up hearing more about sin and less about love? What do we read in the newspapers every day?

I'm not saying that we're not sinful creatures. I can speak only for myself, but my soul looks as if it's been working in a Pennsylvania coal mine for decades. Yet what we've done to ourselves is like a person who owns a beautiful diamond but focuses only on the tiny scratch deep within. There are few perfect diamonds in the world. Each has a flaw. We have spent the whole of human history focusing not on the radiance of the diamond, but obsessing on the blemish. Instead of focusing on love and forgiveness, we've nursed anger and hatred (and those two have become some really unruly children).

God created us to be greater than the angels! *Greater than the angels!* We slipped and fell and scratched ourselves. The cut, the bleeding, however, does not change our original nature. Instead, the enemy has shifted our focus away from the forgiving beauty of God to depravity. If we become what we focus on, then we as *human beings have become everything we were never intended to be.*

Think of it this way. You're driving on the highway, minding your own business, admiring the beautiful sky in front of you. You're keeping up with traffic, and then, out of the corner of your eye, you see a big, naked, ugly, hairy man running along the side of the road giving everyone a thumbs-up. You can't take your eyes off this crazy guy, and in the process your car veers into the next lane and you get into an accident with someone who was so shocked by the big, hairy, naked guy that she didn't know what to do either.

Sin is a big, hairy, chafing, naked guy. We focus more on sin than on God, the giver of love and life, and of that big, bold, beautiful sky in front of us. What happens when we shift our focus?

We crash.

Prayer and meditation help us steal back what it means to be truly human. What does it mean to be truly human? To live knowing that God, through the living person of the Holy Spirit, is inside us and inside everyone else too. To live, to truly live, is to see God in everything.

Everything.

4

Prayer, Meditation, and Contemplation

Let's take a few moments to talk specifically about prayer and meditation, as well as something we haven't really touched on but that is the fruit of both: contemplation. Many people use these three words interchangeably, but while there are similarities among them, there are subtle and not-so-subtle differences among the three that, once understood, can lead to a deepening of your spiritual life.

Prayer, John A. Hardon says, is our "voluntary response to the awareness of God's presence." Essentially, prayer is talking to God—verbally, mentally, or physically—and it can take many different forms, including the following:

Petition: Asking for something
Adoration: Praising God

> Thanksgiving: Expressing gratitude
>
> Expiation: Asking specifically for mercy
>
> Centering: Focusing on a single representative word for God
>
> Mental and meditative: Using the mind to engage God in thought
>
> Contemplation: Gazing on God without words

Prayer can take other forms as well. It can be solitary or done within a community. It can be a letter written to God. It can be a poem or a song or a dance. It can be an outstretched hand helping someone across the street or soothing a young child. It can be your job.

It all depends on your intention. Are you using your actions to communicate with God?

The premise of this book is to practice certain types of formal prayer so that you move toward a state of living in perpetual prayer.

Prayer is a gift for our benefit and is a way of entering a state of intimacy with God. Practically speaking, it is a tool that helps us relieve stress and anxiety, quiet our minds, center our souls, and lead more efficient lives.

I grew up in a house that was well over a hundred years old. This house had a series of cast-iron radiators to keep it warm. During the winter months, the furnace would kick in and the heat and pressure would move the warmed water through the pipes and heat the house (when the furnace wasn't broken).

Every year, though, we had to bleed the air from the pipes, which means we had to open the valves in the radiators to let out all the air that had accumulated in the spring and summer when the heating system wasn't working. It's a pretty simple thing to do. You start the furnace, and then at each radiator you use a special key to open a pressure valve that lets out all the air inside the pipes. If you didn't bleed your pipes every year, it could make for a very dangerous situation. Worst-case scenario: pipes with air in their systems can clang and shake, which can lead to bursting and water damage. Even if it's not that severe, it causes the system to run inefficiently.

Prayer is a lot like bleeding your pipes. You are a powerful, wonderful creation, and God wants you to run as smoothly as possible. Sometimes things don't function correctly. Pockets of discontent and doubt can creep into your system, and once pressure is applied it can make you buckle, shake, and sometimes pop. Prayer allows you to open the valve, to let the air out so that the steam of the Holy Spirit can flow through you in a continuous stream. The more you pray, the more efficient you become in your life.

If prayer is speaking to God, then meditation is essentially, as Richard Foster says in *Celebration of Discipline*, "listening to God." Meditation is listening to God's voice. It also helps us move away from an "it's all about me" inclination to allow us to cultivate a healthy amnesia of self. Meditation is the beginning and the continuation of prayer.

God calls us. We respond. We listen. We respond. We listen. And so on. It's a bit like a dance. God leads. We follow.

Christian meditation, which differs from Eastern meditation, is less about emptying ourselves and more about allowing God to fill us with his desires for us. When we pray, we are usually expressing our needs to God. Meditation allows God to tell us his desires. "What happens in meditation," Foster writes, "is that we create the emotional and spiritual space which allows Christ to construct an inner sanctuary of the heart. . . . Meditation opens the door and, although we are engaging in specific meditative exercises at specific times, the aim is to bring this living reality into all of life."

Yet many of us may have tried meditation and never heard anything. Not one peep from God. Not a word. Not even a clearing of the throat or a sneeze.

Many have written that God speaks in silence. Well, that's great, but that doesn't do me much good. How do I know if God is there if his native tongue is silence?

Experts who study human relationships estimate that nearly eighty percent of all communication is nonverbal. For instance, a friend asks your opinion about the guy she's dating. She says she really wants your viewpoint. So you say, "Sure!" and you let it rip, but as soon as you start talking your friend folds her arms, tightens her jaw, and smiles a smile of a baby whose diaper needs changing.

As you continue speaking, she keeps nodding and saying, "Thank you, I needed to hear this." That's what her mouth is saying, but what is her body saying? She hates you and she wants you to shut up.

If so much of the way we communicate is nonverbal, couldn't God be communicating to us nonverbally? Meditation therefore helps us understand the body language of God. How can we read this? By reading the signs of God's creation around us, by listening to the voices of others and paying attention to how those words affect us emotionally and intellectually. Few of us are ever going to hear God speak in dramatic tones. Most of the time his words come from places you'd never expect—a friend, a bird, a song on your iPod, a billboard, a pothole, an illness, a disappointment—and when it does, you are on your way to a contemplative experience of God.

Not too long ago I was in need of some serious inspiration. I was praying and meditating, and nothing—absolutely nothing—was happening and I was getting very frustrated. I had heard that a favorite priest of mine was back from a long trip to Poland, and I was excited to hear him preach on the upcoming Sunday. I'm not exaggerating when I say that I waited all week to listen to his words, which always brought me comfort and inspiration.

Sunday finally arrived and I was sitting in the pew waiting anxiously for the homily. Just as the priest finished reading the Gospel and started to preach, a baby two rows behind me started to cry.

He didn't stop.

This baby had some set of lungs. I remember turning and looking at the parents as if to say, "Please take your spawn and leave! Some of us need to listen to this guy." Coward that I am, I said nothing and just tried to listen through the screaming.

I couldn't pay attention to the priest. I tried. I really did, but I couldn't hear anything except the wail of this child.

I started to get angry and, God forgive me, an instant of hate flashed into my heart. All I wanted to do was to get out of the spiritual dark place I was in, and my one salvation was this homily. I couldn't make out a single word.

When the priest was done, guess what? Yes, the baby stopped crying.

I left church soon thereafter. Dejected and angry.

That night I had a dream.

In this dream, which is a bit of a recurring dream, I was standing before Jesus (or at least my image of Jesus—he looks a little bit like Michael Landon with a beard), and I asked him, "What is the meaning of life?"

Jesus looked at me, smiled, opened his mouth, and out came a cry of a baby.

I woke up.

I wasn't in church that day to hear God in the priest's voice. I was there to hear God in the cries of a child.

That moment after waking wasn't an intellectual knowing but an emotional experiencing of God. It was a feeling. As I lay in the dark of the night, I felt strange. I felt changed, but I couldn't tell you how. It was only after reflecting the next day that I realized it: upon waking, I had walked through the door to contemplation.

There are many different definitions of contemplation. We often confuse the word with meditation. In the secular sense, this is fine, but in Christian spirituality, the two are very different. According to our friend Hardon, St. Augustine called contemplation the enjoyable admiration of perceived truth, St. Bernard called it the elevation of mind resting on God, and St. Thomas called it a simple divine truth that produces love. In his book *New Seeds of Contemplation* Thomas Merton offers his own explanation:

> [Contemplation] is the highest expression of man's intellectual and spiritual self. . . . It is spiritual wonder. It is spontaneous awe at the sacredness of life, of being. It is gratitude of life, for awareness and for being. It is a vivid realization of the fact that life and being in us proceed from an invisible, transcendent and infinitely abundant Source. Contemplation is, above all, awareness of the reality of that Source.

In its essence, contemplation is an experience of God that comes from God. It's something ineffable, and to try to put it into words will always end in disappointment (which doesn't mean we shouldn't try). And though we can prepare ourselves for contemplation by praying and meditating, we cannot force contemplation to occur.

You and I can pray. We can pray together. We can pray alone. We can pray with our minds or with our bodies. We can say words or we can be silent. We can also meditate and relax the body. These are things we can work out. These are exercises we can do. Contemplation, on the other hand, can't be *done*. It's something that happens to us.

It is a gift from God.

Contemplation is grace.

Part Two: The Prayer Exercises

The old man spoke:

"You are like a person who has waited his entire life to see a painting in a museum. You finally get your chance to travel, to go to this place you have been dreaming about. You enter, you find where the painting is, and you walk to the room. Before you enter, you take a deep breath and then walk in. The painting is to your right, and you automatically move as close to it as you possibly can without touching it. Certainly if the curator and not the security guard was in the room, you would be told to step away. But you are here. You are looking at the painting you've waited your whole life to see and you can see the gentle curves of the brush, the color of a patch of the piece. You are so close you can even see the slightly visible fingerprints of the artist that are barely distinguishable from the brushstroke.

"Something catches your eye, though, and you turn around and see another man, a distinguished and gentle man standing in the middle of the room observing the same painting as you are, but from a distance. He must be viewing you too because you've become a part of the painting yourself, you're so close to it. You are intrigued and you want to see what he sees, so you move closer to him. Standing shoulder to shoulder (you're a bit shorter than he is), you look around and you see the painting you've always wanted to see, but from a different perspective. It is beautiful, but so are all these other paintings in the room—the paintings you missed."

5

Learning to Listen

This book attempts to explain, through definition and personal reflections, certain types of prayer, and it offers some guided meditations that will, we hope, through divine love, prepare you for an experience of God.

However, we do not have control over how God will respond to us. Some of us may pray not just for fifteen minutes a day, but for hours during the day, and still never have God respond to us the way we want him to. There is only one guarantee in the spiritual life: *God wants us to experience him in this life; we just don't have control over how this is going to happen.* We can, though, be diligent in our faith and till the soil of our hearts and souls to make it fertile ground in which the seed of God's love can take root.

Furthermore, this book is not a comprehensive lexicon on prayer and meditation. It leans heavily toward three types of prayer: breath, centering, and *lectio divina* (praying with Scripture). I have spotlighted these three because I believe we live in a world of great thinkers. By this I don't mean that everyone is a pocket-protected rocket scientist or a pipe-smoking, tweed-wearing intellectual philosopher; rather, I mean that humans are always thinking. We may be thinking about God or about a bill we need to pay. We may be thinking of someone we love or plotting revenge against an enemy. We think about our health, our jobs, the economy, our car that needs brakes, whether or not we should buy new shoes or paint the house. For most of us, if we're not speaking with our mouths, we're rambling in our heads.

While thinking is important, too much of it, focused on the wrong things, can lead to depression, anger, and jealousy, to name just a few. As a society, as humanity, we all need to stop thinking so much. Prayer through breath, centering, and *lectio divina* can help us silence the mind and relax the body.

In addition, I have included intermittent personal reflections and short exercises that I hope will assist you with your prayer journey.

None of these prayers and exercises will take more than a couple of minutes to perform (some take only a matter of seconds), but in order to become spiritually proficient, you must use the art of daily repetition. A great baseball pitcher doesn't throw a ball once a day. He throws it hundreds of times. A dancer doesn't practice a five-second move two minutes a day; she does it for hours. You have life not because your heart beats once, but because it repeats that action over and over again.

Before we move on, just a few words on spiritual dryness and boredom.

There are going to be moments when you feel absolutely nothing on your spiritual journey. Frustration can follow. Anger can follow as well. You may become uninterested and fed up. Do not fall into this trap. Just as a person can walk around during a cloudy day and still return home with a sunburn, there will be times when you do not feel the effects of spiritual exercises. This does not mean they are not working. This is where real faith comes into play. It's easy to have faith when we feel God is speaking to us, when we're excited about the journey and what we might discover. But the true test of faith is how we respond when God is silent and we grow confused over what that silence means.

A few years ago, a book was published about Mother Teresa. This collection of her writings describes how alienated she felt from God during all her years of service. Many people were shocked by this. How could someone who seemed to be so deeply religious and obedient to God say such things?

The only way to answer that is to ask if you've ever been in love with someone desperately. Your world revolves around this person and you want your beloved to respond to you in a certain way, but this person never does. Now, this person could love you just as much as you love, but because he or she never responds to you *in the way you expect*, you feel isolated, alone, vacant. Loneliness wraps its dark wings around you, and you feel as if you're going to die. This can happen between lovers, husbands and wives, parents and children.

This can happen between you and God.

Many people say you shouldn't have expectations in your spiritual life. I don't believe this. Moses had expectations—so did Jonah, so did Paul, so did Jesus. We should expect God to answer us, but we have to acquiesce *to the way* he responds.

He will respond, but watch out what you wish for, because once you get him started, you can't shut him up.

∞

For those times when spiritual dryness tempts you to give up, Richard Foster, in his book *Celebration of Discipline*, offers these words of comfort: "You must not be discouraged. . . . There is a progression on the spiritual life, and it is wise to have some experience with lesser peaks before trying to tackle the Mt. Everest of the soul. So be patient with yourself. . . . You will be going against the tide, but take heart; your task is of immense worth."

And to quote the Gospel of Matthew:

Ask, and it will be given to you; search, and you will find; knock, and the door will be opened for you. For everyone who asks receives, and everyone who searches finds, and for everyone who knocks, the door will be opened. Is there anyone among you who, if your child asks for bread, will give a stone? Or if the child asks for a fish, will give a snake? If you then, who are evil, know how to give good gifts to your children, how much more will your Father in heaven give good things to those who ask him!

In everything do to others as you would have them do to you; for this is the law and the prophets. (Matthew 7:7–12)

Let's begin.

6

Breath Prayer

All life begins with a single breath, and so we begin these spiritual exercises by focusing on our breathing. Why? Besides the fact that deep, controlled, focused breathing is beneficial to our physical health, it also helps us shift our attention from whatever is on our minds—our problems, our desires, our responsibilities—to the gift we received from God at birth: our breath.

The following simple exercise is a form of preprayer or premeditation. It's a way of clearing your mind and directing your concentration toward God, and it's preparation for the first exercise we'll discuss, the Jesus Prayer:

- Find a comfortable place that's relatively quiet. Sit up straight or lie down and just relax for a few moments. Take a deep breath in and a deep breath out. Focus on your breath going in and out and repeat these words:

- ○ Breathe in: "I am breathing in God."
- ○ Breathe out: "God is breathing through me."
- ○ Breathe in: "I am breathing in Jesus."
- ○ Breathe out: "Jesus is breathing through me."
- ○ Breathe in: "I am breathing in Holy Spirit."
- ○ Breathe out: "I am breathing out the Holy Spirit."

- Repeat until you feel your body and mind start to relax.

You can use your breath as a tool for any prayer or meditation. One way of using breathing is in the reciting of the Our Father. This allows us to focus on the words more clearly and will be used later on in this book when we talk about centering prayer and *lectio divina*. This is a simple rhythm you can use:

- Breathe in and say: "Our Father,"
- Breathe out and say: "who art in heaven,"
- Breathe in and say: "hallowed be thy name."
- Breathe out and say: "Thy Kingdom come,"
- Breathe in and say: "thy will be done,"
- Breathe out and say: "on earth"
- Breathe in and say: "as it is in heaven."
- Breathe out and say: "Give us this day"
- Breathe in and say: "our daily bread,"

- Breathe out and say: "and forgive us our trespasses,"
- Breathe in and say: "as we forgive those"
- Breathe out and say: "who trespass against us."
- Breathe in and say: "And lead us not into temptation"
- Breathe out and say: "but deliver us from evil."
- Breathe in and say: "Amen."

Breath Prayer Exercise #1: The Jesus Prayer

The Jesus Prayer originated among the Desert Fathers, a group of Christian holy men who lived in the arid regions of Egypt somewhere around the fifth century. It is a simple meditative prayer and one that has been popularized by the classic nineteenth-century spiritual text known as *The Way of a Pilgrim.* That book, written by an anonymous Russian author, chronicles a simple peasant's search for God and how saying this prayer helped him see God in all things.

My introduction to the prayer, however, didn't come from that book, but rather from *Franny and Zooey*, a book by J. D. Salinger, the beloved author of *The Catcher in the Rye*. In this book, Franny and Zooey are sister and brother, and the book is essentially two long discussions about the meaning of life. Franny, who is having a difficult time with her boyfriend, has picked up a copy of *The Way of the Pilgrim* and begins saying the Jesus Prayer to herself: "Lord Jesus Christ, have mercy on me." She repeats this prayer until she enters a certain trance-like state.

You can do that, I told myself when I was done reading. Salinger's story led me to *The Way of the Pilgrim*, and it was those words of the prayer that set me off on a journey of the Spirit I never thought possible.

But what exactly is this prayer? The author of *The Way of the Pilgrim* describes it this way:

> The Jesus Prayer is a continuous, uninterrupted call on the holy name of Jesus Christ with the lips, mind, and heart; and in the awareness of His abiding presence it is a plea for his undertakings, in all places, at all times, even in sleep. . . . Anyone who becomes accustomed to this prayer will experience great comfort as well as the need to say it continuously. He will become accustomed to it in such a degree that he will not be able to do without it and eventually the Prayer will of itself flow in him.

At the heart of the prayer is repetition. You don't just say the Jesus Prayer once; you say it a hundred times, a thousand times, ten thousand times. You can say it before you go to sleep, in the moments after you wake up, when you're waiting at a traffic light, or standing in line at a grocery store. The prayer is made up of two parts. The first is an acknowledgment of the Savior: *Lord Jesus Christ.* The second is a simple petition: *Have mercy on me.* Try this:

- Breathe in for a count of four.
- Hold for a count of four.
- Breathe out for a count of four.
- Hold for a count of four.
- Repeat this four times.
- On the fifth time, begin your prayer and follow this breathing pattern:
  - Breathe in and repeat: "Lord Jesus Christ."
  - Hold.
  - Breathe out and repeat: "Have mercy on me."
  - Hold.
  - Repeat.

Breath Prayer Exercise #2:
Sacred Heart of Jesus

This prayer uses the form of the Jesus Prayer but substitutes a different image, that of the sacred heart of Jesus. Here we picture Jesus's enthusiastic, glowing heart, filled with the healing power of the Holy Spirit emanating from his chest. This is a prayer to increase faith and to aid healing.

Imagine the Holy Spirit flowing through the prism of Jesus's divine heart. The light of divine love shines on you and brings you increased peace and warmth. It's important to focus on the image, to feel the warming effects of the Spirit touching you, enveloping you, increasing your awareness that you are one with God.

This prayer follows the same rhythm as the Jesus Prayer:

- Breathe in to the count of four.
- Hold for a count of four.
- Breathe out for a count of four.
- Hold for a count of four.
- Do this four times.
- On the fifth time, begin your prayer and follow this breathing pattern:
    ○ Breathe in and repeat: "Sacred heart of Jesus."
    ○ Hold.
    ○ Breathe out and repeat: "I trust in you."
    ○ Hold and repeat.

Breath Prayer Exercise #3: Come, Holy Spirit, Come

This prayer is a petition for your increased awareness of the Holy Spirit in your life. The Spirit is ever present, flowing through each and every one of us, tying together all of creation. Yet we forget or don't realize the sometimes subtle movement of this divine person who is always present inside us. We just need to let the Spirit do its job and affect how we live:

- Breathe in to the count of four.
- Hold for a count of four.
- Breathe out for a count of four.
- Hold for a count of four.
- Do this four times.
- On the fifth time, begin your prayer and follow this breathing pattern:
  ◦ Breathe in and repeat: "Come, Holy Spirit, come."
  ◦ Hold.
  ◦ Breathe out and repeat: "Come, Holy Spirit, come."
  ◦ Hold.
  ◦ Repeat.

Breath Prayer Exercise #4: Only Say the Word and I Shall Be Healed

These words, "Only say the word and I shall be healed," a paraphrase of the words spoken by the centurion to Jesus in Matthew's Gospel and intoned during the Catholic Mass, is a great way of asking God to bring spiritual, mental, physical, and emotional healing into your life:

- Breathe in to the count of four.

- Hold for a count of four.
- Breathe out for a count of four.
- Hold for a count of four.
- Do this four times.
- On the fifth time, begin your prayer and follow this breathing pattern:
  - Breathe in and repeat: "Only say the word and I shall be healed."
  - Hold.
  - Breathe out and repeat: "Only say the word and I shall be healed."
  - Hold.
  - Repeat.

7

Centering Prayer

Centering prayer, like the Jesus Prayer, dates back to the time of the Desert Fathers and is a core teaching in *The Cloud of Unknowing*, a guide on how to pray that was written by an anonymous English monk sometime during the fourteenth century. This monk wrote: "This is what you are to do: lift your heart up to the Lord with a gentle stirring of love, desiring him for his own sake and not his gifts. Center all your attention and desire on him and let this be the sole concern of your mind and heart."

It is a form of prayer that gained popularity in the twentieth century partly because of Trappist monks, including M. Basil Pennington, who describes it in his book *Centering Prayer* as "a simple method—a technique, if you like that term—to get in touch with what *is*."

In this prayer, through the grace of God we focus our attention on the Holy Spirit, who lives within each and every one of us. How do we do this? By attempting to evacuate all the extraneous thoughts in our hearts and to focus on a single representative word for that indwelling—for example, *God*, *Jesus*, *Spirit*, *love*, *faith*, or *strength*. It is a quiet form of prayer, one we do individually and in solitude.

Solitude, though, can be found in the strangest of places.

Between the hours of 4:00 and 7:00 p.m. on any given weekday, the streets around Pennsylvania Station in New York City are crowded with tens of thousands of weary—and during the summertime, sweaty—people with one goal in mind: to get the heck out of the city and go home. It was on one of those ordinary commuter days in the middle of a hot summer, standing in a swarm of people waiting for the traffic light to change at the intersection of Thirty-Fourth and Seventh, that I happened to glance at the sandaled foot of a young woman who had the word *love* tattooed on her big toe.

Her big toe?

What in this young woman's mind compelled her to do such a thing? I'm not against tattoos, but that had to hurt! Why the word *love* on her foot? As I imagined what it must have felt like to be stabbed innumerous times by a tiny needle, I was swept up in a frenzy of anxious commuters ready to trample me to paralysis if I didn't cross the street.

The tattooed woman walked off and quickly disappeared into the crowd. As I descended into the mouth of Penn Station, I couldn't get the image of the love tattoo out of my mind. Soon thereafter a strange thing started to happen. Even though I was caught in the rush of the late-afternoon commute, the world around me started slowing down and I began noticing tattoos everywhere.

There were Celtic designs, stars, Our Lady of Guadalupe, a birdcage, Elvis, a flag, a fish, a snake, and single words on different body parts on various people: *Mom*, *hope*, *faith*, *justice*. It seemed that just about every person in New York that day, from young teenagers to grandparents, was walking around with a tattoo.

What was going on here? Why had so many people decided to paint their bodies? Was it just a trendy thing to do? Or was there something else going on?

We live in a transient world. People are born. People age. People die. Some lose their hair. Some get fat, then skinny, and fat again. They learn something new and then they forget it. They lose things. They find others. Houses are built.

Apartments are torn down. Some days you have faith. Other days you don't.

Other days you don't even want to hear the word *God* mentioned: The toy you loved so much as a child is thrown out by a parent. The job to which you dedicated so much of your life is eliminated, and you have to start all over again at the age of fifty. The girl you loved so much as a teenager breaks your heart, runs off with the drummer in your best friend's band, traipses off to France, returns with a new haircut, a nose ring, and a designer bag, and moves to Minneapolis to become a TV weather woman because she loved *The Mary Tyler Moore Show* and always wanted to stand in the middle of a busy street and throw her beret in the air.

In our ever-changing world we desire permanence. Your dog may leave you one day, but a tattoo, well, that's forever. The surge in tattooing, while maybe just the cool thing of the moment, seems to be indicative of a yearning to live in the presence of something everlasting. This longing to experience the eternal is at the heart of centering prayer.

The girl with the toe tattoo was my first encounter with this type of devotion, even though I didn't know it at the time. In centering prayer, you choose one word with sacred significance—*peace, faith, joy, Spirit, God, Jesus*—and focus your attention on that particular word, repeating it to yourself until, through the grace of God, you begin to experience an internal shift. On that day, my word was *love*.

As I sat down on the always-crowded 5:36 p.m. eastbound train to Long Island, snug between a sweaty guy with a hairnet and a woman who texted her BFF every thirty seconds, I started focusing on love, repeating it to myself. As the train lurched out of the station, my mind started to wander a bit—I was focusing on love, but then other things would enter my mind: worries, work, family, stop signs, light bulbs, the Yankees, and Pez dispensers. Then my mind shifted back to love.

Love. God. Love. Christ. Love. Mother Teresa. The word *love* in graffiti on a wall in Queens, New York. This homeless woman I passed on the street every day on my way to work. *Love. Resurrection. Love. God. Love.* Soon I experienced a tiny movement of the heart and I fell into a steady rhythm, and everything around me started to fall away. I couldn't feel the heat of sweaty dude next to me, and I no longer heard texting girl next to me chewing her gum like a horse. All the noise in the train vanished, and I was lulled into this state where love was the primary focus. I even stopped thinking of pop stars and cumulus arcus.

Centering Prayer Exercise: Find the Word in Your Heart

- Find a comfortable place where you won't be disturbed.

- Perform the premeditation breathing technique to calm you, repeating the Our Father as you consciously breathe in God and breathe out fear and stress.

- Begin with a short prayer of your own choosing, asking God to guide you in your focus. Ask God to help you quiet your mind and reinvigorate your heart.

- Find the word that comes to your heart. If nothing comes, focus on the word *God*.

- Breathe the word in.

- Breathe the word out.

- Stay still, repeating the word to yourself, focusing the word in your heart, which seems to grow stronger with each beat. Then let the word go and sit in its presence as you would an old friend.

- Let it rest in you.

8

Lectio Divina

Lectio divina, a form of centering prayer, is Latin for "holy reading," in this case, the holy reading of Scripture. It is, as well-respected spiritual director Adele Ahlberg Calhoun writes, "a way of entering deeply into the text with a heart alert to a unique and personal word from God. Words and verses that catch our attention become invitations to be with God in prayer."

A few years ago, I was going through yet another rough patch in my relationship with God and we (God and I) decided that we would go on retreat to try and recharge my spiritual batteries. Obviously, God's batteries were fine. Mine needed a power plant connected to some heavy-duty jumper cables to get them up and running.

Looking back, I see it was akin to a married couple who, having grown tired of each other, decide to go to the Poconos for a weekend—maybe get back some of that romance they'd lost with familiarity. Picture one driving the car, talking ceaselessly, while the other stares blankly out the window at mountains and rest stops, worrying about work, questioning his or her existence, resting in self-loathing, thinking of failure and defeat, hearing nothing except the sound teachers make in the Charlie Brown cartoons.

The retreat was, spiritually speaking, a disaster from the start. I wasn't into it. I tried. I went through the motions—we spent time alone, I spoke, God spoke; we went for walks; we sat in front of the fireplace; we read books (I was reading Paulo Coelho's *The Fifth Mountain* about Elijah; God, of course, was reading the newspaper, the world section); we ate together. It went nowhere. I was there physically—and I really was trying—but I just wasn't feeling an emotional connection.

I went through this whole scenario in my head where I dumped God in a public place so there wouldn't be too much of a scene. There would be tears. There would be anger. Ultimately it was the best thing to do. I pictured myself valiantly walking away and swearing I would never turn back.

In the end, I chickened out and decided I would dump God via e-mail.

I walked to my room, switched on the laptop I brought with me, and started to type "Dear God," when the screen started flashing and I realized I needed to charge the battery. I went to my suitcase and soon realized I had left the power cable at home. While I was searching, the screen went black. Ugh. I then decided I needed to be out of that room, so I picked up my Bible and went for a walk.

We were staying at St. Ignatius Retreat House in New York. The grounds are small but beautiful—tree-filled and green with a few benches—and that day there was a warm breeze blowing from the east. I plopped myself down and opened the Bible.

I started to read. Nothing. *I give up.* I put the Bible next to me on the bench and the wind surged. The pages started flapping and I started smiling. "Up to your old tricks again," I said out loud. "Okay, you want to play biblical roulette, let's see what you got, old man!"

The wind blew the pages to the left and then to the right and then to the left again. It all sounded like a gambler shuffling cards. When the wind died down, I looked over and the Bible had come to rest on the story of the talents.

"Okay, you have my attention," I said. With that I started to read.

The Parable of the Talents

For it is as if a man, going on a journey, summoned his slaves and entrusted his property to them; to one he gave five talents, to another two, to another one, to each according to his ability. Then he went away. The one who had received the five talents went off at once and traded with them, and made five more talents. In the same way, the one who had the two talents made two more talents. But the one who had received the one talent went off and dug a hole in the ground and hid his master's money. After a long time the master of those slaves came and settled accounts with them. Then the one who had received the five talents came forward, bringing five more talents, saying, "Master, you handed over to me five talents; see, I have made five more talents." His master said to him, "Well done, good and trustworthy slave; you have been trustworthy in a few things, I will put you in charge of many things; enter into the joy of your master." And the one with the two talents also came forward, saying, "Master, you handed over to me two talents; see, I have made two more talents." His master said to him, "Well done, good and trustworthy slave; you have been trustworthy in a few things, I will put you in charge of many things; enter into the joy of your master." Then the one who had received the one talent also came forward, saying, "Master, I knew that you were a harsh man, reaping where you did not sow, and gathering where you did not scatter seed; so I was afraid, and I went and hid

your talent in the ground. Here you have what is yours."
But his master replied, "You wicked and lazy slave! You
knew, did you, that I reap where I did not sow, and gather
where I did not scatter? Then you ought to have invested
my money with the bankers, and on my return I would
have received what was my own with interest. So take the
talent from him, and give it to the one with the ten talents.
For to all those who have, more will be given, and they
will have an abundance; but from those who have nothing, even what they have will be taken away. As for this
worthless slave, throw him into the outer darkness, where
there will be weeping and gnashing of teeth." (Matthew
25:14–30)

The word *talent* stayed with me, putting its arm around my
shoulder, and just sat there as I went through a range of emotions: fear, hope, shame, love. I then remembered the story of
Elijah and the wind and the whisper:

He said, "Go out and stand on the mountain before the
LORD, for the LORD is about to pass by." Now there was a
great wind, so strong that it was splitting mountains and
breaking rocks in pieces before the LORD, but the LORD
was not in the wind; and after the wind an earthquake, but
the LORD was not in the earthquake; and after the earthquake a fire, but the LORD was not in the fire; and after
the fire a sound of sheer silence. When Elijah heard it, he
wrapped his face in his mantle and went out and stood

at the entrance of the cave. Then there came a voice to him that said, "What are you doing here, Elijah?" (1 Kings 19:11–13)

My heart answered. "Forgive me."

Lectio Divina Exercise: Praying with Scripture

1. Make sure you have a Bible or a sacred piece of writing to read.

2. Breathe: As I've mentioned before, it is a good idea to begin any prayer and meditation by taking a few moments to center yourself and become conscious of your breathing. Find a patch of silence inside you and go there.

3. Read the Scripture passage. Try to take your time as you read the text. Even people familiar with certain stories are frequently surprised by the words or phrases that stand out during different readings. If something takes hold of you, stay with it. Allow your mind to quiet further and allow your soul to explore those words that have meaning for you. What is it about those particular phrases that speak to you?

4. Meditate. Pause again and let the words settle into you. Enter the scene in this sacred reading and begin pondering. Gently reflect on what you've read, prayed, and

experienced. Do you feel anxious? Do you feel afraid? Are you happy or sad? What does this scene mean to you? If you were there that day, what would you have done?

5. While you are doing this, take time to relax your mind and try not to think of anything in particular. It's a hard thing to do, but give God time to respond. During this time you may become distracted or bored. Your mind may race around a million little things: bills, commitments, family members, your dog, the color you want to paint your bathroom. Your back may hurt or your backside get numb. This is normal and is all part of the process. Allow the experience to occur, acknowledge it either verbally or mentally, then shift your focus back to your prayer and meditation. Do this as often as necessary. The more you enter into this direct communication with God, the easier it will become, as Henri Nouwen wrote in *The Wounded Healer*, to "make visible what was hidden, make touchable what was unreachable."

6. Pray. Speak to God about what you're experiencing. Be open to God's response to you.

7. Drop all words and allow yourself to be with God in the picture or idea of the text. Continue to focus on your breathing.

Part Three: Encountering God Exercises

A man stood outside a church in the middle of a busy city and watched as passersby went about their daily business. Many were shuffling off to work, others were walking around in shorts with newspapers and brown paper bags, and still others seemed lost and in need of directions. Around noon, the man looked up at the tall steeple and fixed his gaze upon the thin iron cross that sat on the top. Every once in a while a man on his way to lunch or a woman on her way to the drugstore for cotton balls would slow down and look up too. If the person lingered for a moment, the man would ask, "What is the Holy Spirit?" Many people said nothing and took his words as their cue to move on. Some said, "I don't know." Others said words like *God, Jesus, grass, smoke, fire, energy, a new line of sports shoes.* This went on for hours.

As the sun began to set, casting the street in the colors of Sri Lankan silk, and after hours of staring upward, his neck stiff and pinched, the man turned his gaze to the street. Walking toward him was a beautiful woman in a sundress. With the sun shining on her she looked as if she radiated phosphorus.

"What is the Holy Spirit?" the man asked.

The beautiful woman smiled, looking like an angel from God, raised her hand, her fingers painted in Technicolor, and slapped his face with the strength of a small army.

"That's the Holy Spirit," she said and walked away.

The man, his cheek burning with the fire of Pentecost, knew exactly what she meant.

9

The Holy Pressure

What the world is missing now is not a new religion, or for that matter, as many would argue, a new atheism. It's not missing a new brilliant technology for whitening teeth. It's most certainly not missing another cable TV station. Though poverty, lack of food, AIDS, war, and depleting energy sources are all major concerns in the twenty-first century, and solutions to these crises are needed urgently, something else is missing from our world. Something that is so important that if you were to have it you could change your life right now. Not only that, *you could change the world.*

This thing is in short supply even though it's present among us right now. You can see the effects of this shortage in the eyes of many people you see every day—from the checkout clerk at a Wal-Mart in Tennessee to the stockbroker on Wall Street in New York City.

You know what we're critically missing now, more than anything else in the world?

Enthusiasm.

That inflammation of the soul, that fire in our hearts, that passion that drives us to new and glorious heights.

Many would disagree with me and argue that enthusiasm is all around us. Certainly if you've ever been to a football game or a rock concert, you haven't just seen or heard enthusiasm. You've *experienced* its power. What about wedding parties? Well, yes, those are some excited people at these gatherings, especially the drunk ones (people to this day still talk about my wedding). What about the stock market and all those people in the pit, flailing their arms and buying or selling? All those people are enthusiastic, right?

And what about all those *bad* people? It's certainly true that we live in a time when religious fanaticism is a very big concern. Enthusiasm can be about being passionate for a cause, and while this might sound like a political or ideological statement, I assure you it is not. I am not advocating zealotry or fanaticism, both of which abuse enthusiasm's essence and exploit it the way pornography exploits sex.

What some people take for enthusiasm is little more than misdirected energy—the way, the night before a test, a normally studious schoolboy jacks himself up on soda and chocolate and spends his time bouncing off the walls instead of putting his nose in a book. What you have the next day is a tired, dehydrated young person staring at an almost blank page in class, mentally kicking himself in the rear for not having spent time doing what he should have done the night before—studying. The boy was certainly filled with energy, but none of us would argue that he was being enthusiastic.

Then what do I mean by *enthusiasm*? According to *Webster's Collegiate Dictionary*, the word comes from the Greek *enthousiasmos*, to be inspired from God (bringing together the roots *en-* and *theos*), and it means to have "a belief in special revelations of the Holy Spirit."

What the world is missing now isn't misdirected energy, it is an outpouring—a flowing awareness—of the living presence of the Holy Spirit that exists in each and every one of us.

Imagine for a moment nothing except your kitchen or bathroom sink. Imagine that your sink has a single handle that you can turn on and off rather easily. Behind the wall is a series of interconnected, high-pressure pipes that bring the water into your home from a larger source, a reservoir or a water tower or a local water station. When the water is shut off at your sink, a tiny valve closes that prevents water from flowing. When that valve is closed, the water behind it is under pressure. Extreme pressure. It's sitting there in that pipe and wants badly to be unleashed. Yet you control when the water is turned on, and you also determine how powerful the flow is.

The water is always there. The potential is always just a few centimeters behind a tiny, powerful valve.

You may lift the handle only slightly to get a trickle of water as you wet your toothbrush. You may lift the valve all the way to get a powerful steady stream of water in order to wash your dishes.

Imagine that water is the Holy Spirit, and imagine there is a faucet connected to your heart. Focus on the heart and focus on this faucet, which is connected to a pipe that contains the Holy Spirit. The Spirit is under intense pressure. He's pushing on the valve of your faucet heart. You can feel that pressure when you wake up in the morning, throughout your day at work, when you are stuck in traffic, in the moments before sleep.

It's the holy pressure.

Keep this image in your mind. Turn on the faucet.

The Holy Spirit Exercise

How is the Spirit flowing through you? Or is the Spirit flowing through you? Is the valve in your heart open or closed? Are you living with the valve open all the way to let the Spirit flow strongly and steadily through your life? Or are you living each day drip by drip by drip?

However you answer that question, I want you to reach inside your heart and increase the flow by lifting the handle of the faucet. If the valve was totally shut off and nothing was getting through, I want you to open the faucet slightly and pray this simple prayer: "Flow through me, Holy Spirit. Flow through me."

If the Spirit has been dripping through you, I want you to increase the stream in your life. Pray this simple prayer: "Flow through me, Spirit. Flow through me."

Repeat one thousand times daily.

10

Heroes and Arks

My five-year-old son wants to be a superhero. Not just one superhero, but many: Spiderman, Superman, Batman, Green Lantern, a Power Ranger, and most recently Luigi, the plumber-superhero brother of Mario from the *Super Mario Bros.* video games. He'll dress up like these characters and act out different scenarios. Sometimes he's saving a princess or knocking out a bad guy (usually me—I'm the villain all the time). He wants to save the world.

I love superheroes too, and I wanted to introduce him to one of my favorites, Indiana Jones—the archaeologist and adventurer from those great action-packed movies by Steven Spielberg and George Lucas. After a long dinnertime debate with my wife about some of the content, I threw the movie *Raiders of the Lost Ark* into the DVD player, sat my son down, and said, "Okay, you have to watch this."

He was riveted.

So was I. Not just for the awesome action sequences, but because this movie took on a whole new meaning in my life.

Do you know the story of *Raiders of the Lost Ark*? In the years before World War II, our hero, Indiana Jones, is asked to track down the famed and legendary Ark of the Covenant before the Nazis locate it to use for devious purposes. Now, the ark is this box that holds the Ten Commandments, the stone tablets that God gave to Moses and that the ancient Hebrews treasured and carried with them wherever they went. At some point in history the ark went missing and has been sought after ever since, because it is said that whoever wields the ark will have great power—the power of God.

As I was watching the movie, my mind started to race.

The Ten Commandments were God's covenant with the Israelites, an agreement between the Lord and his people: "Follow my commandments and you follow me and you will be called blessed." This was the Word of God, and there was great power in those words.

That agreement lasted for thousands of years, but then along came this guy Jesus. He became the new covenant, not just with one group of people, but a covenant for all people. But Jesus didn't live long; he died a relatively young man. Yet before he died he promised to leave behind an advocate, a *paraclete*, an adviser who would be the living presence of God in all our lives. That protector was and is the Holy Spirit.

After Jesus's death, resurrection, and ascension, the Holy Spirit makes his presence known to the apostles and in turn becomes a living fire that burns in each and every one of us. This means that each of us carries within us the Word of God, the new agreement, the new covenant. This in turn means that each of us is an ark of the covenant. Each of us is a container for the great and awesome power of God. This does not make us God, but God is present in every one of us. Every one of us contains the awesome power of God.

"Now," you might be saying, "don't talk about such things. God doesn't want us to be powerful; he wants us to be humble. Humility is nothing more than knowing your place."

You and I are not God; we are human beings with God living in us. Yet too often humility becomes confused with low self-esteem. Over our lifetimes, many of us have come to believe that in order to show humility to God, we need to think of ourselves as lowly, sinful, base creatures. Blame religion. Blame society. Blame philosophers. Blame our families.

This is not what God wants for us. Certainly, God wants us to be aware of our sinfulness, but God calls us to be heroes, to be strong, to help save ourselves, and in turn to save the lives of others.

Jesus redefines for us what it means to be truly human. For thousands of years we lived as children of Adam, the fallen man. Jesus, through the miracle of his resurrection, calls us to be sons and daughters of the blessed Trinity, to live a new life and in the process to engage in a constant redefinition of what it means to be human. Jesus is our model for this new interpretation. Jesus is the hero to be emulated.

What is a hero? A hero is a person who takes action to help people. That is what the Holy Spirit calls us to do. When the Spirit descended on Mary after the angel Gabriel told her she was to be the mother of Jesus, what did she do? She took action. She packed her things and journeyed to her cousin Elizabeth. To do what? To serve her. When the Holy Spirit descended on Jesus after his baptism by John, what did he do? He took action and did what? He began his ministry and began serving. When the Spirit descended on the apostles at Pentecost, what did they do? They relinquished fear and began serving the people. Not just one group of people but all people, of all nations.

We too are called to serve, to not be afraid. With the Holy Spirit already dwelling in us, there is no time to waste. We need to take action now and assist those around us, whether it's a family member, a friend, a coworker, a stranger on the street, our environment, our nation, or our world.

How Can I Serve? Exercise

Each morning, as part of your prayer, ask God this very important question: "How can I serve?" Then be quiet and allow God to answer. You may not get an answer right away, but keep asking that question. Allow these words, "How can I serve?" to become for you like the Jesus Prayer, words spoken to yourself during the day and through the night. Let the words become your breath.

11

Feel It, See It, Taste It, Touch It, Smell It

If you're a Christian and have attended church for a number of years, you've probably heard the following, oh, maybe a million times: "God loved us so much that he sent his only son to us so he could save us from our sins."

Well, that's just great. They are important words for Christians. They formulate a basic tenet of our faith. Yet what do those words really mean to you and to me? Even though we have images here—*God*, *love*, *son*, *sins*—they are just words, abstractions.

Conversion, a movement toward God, happens when the words become flesh to us. Jesus is, as John's Gospel says, the Word. Yet he is just a concept until he becomes flesh, until the Son becomes man. When God takes on the role of divine human in our history, that is when stuff gets good. The words need to become flesh. They need to be touched. We need to feel them and to have our hearts breathe life into them.

Too much of our faith is caught up in abstraction, and these abstractions end up becoming theological clichés: "Jesus died for our sins," "God loves you." Yes, this is great, thank you, but what does this mean to us as human beings?

One of the problems with the human condition is that unless something is happening to us directly, it's very hard to feel sympathy or compassion. This is not to say that there aren't sympathetic or compassionate people in the world. But if I have a headache, no matter how painful a headache it is, you cannot experience that headache for me. That is my own personal pain. It does not involve you unless I become angry or rude or ask you for an aspirin. Then it affects you.

For us to be compassionate, we need, even if only momentarily, to imagine we are suffering the pain. Usually people who have suffered are the most compassionate because they know what it's like. This is the Jesus problem and why so many of us have a hard time with our faith. We cannot *feel* all this love that our religion tells us we should be feeling.

One way of transcending this predicament is to engage the imagination, to move beyond words and into images. One of the easiest ways of doing this is to select a favorite passage of Scripture, read it a few times to familiarize yourself with the basic story, and then use your imagination to visualize yourself as deeply in the scene as humanly possible. You can imagine that you are either the main character—maybe Jesus or Mary—or a bystander watching from the sidelines. Then you engage your senses.

Imagination Exercise

Suppose you pick the scene in Exodus where God reveals himself to Moses through a burning bush. Open your heart and use your senses: look, listen, feel, smell, and taste the scene and make it as real as you can. Imagine Mount Sinai and the vistas Moses sees when he looks out across the land. Imagine what Moses looks like. What is he wearing? Are his sandals worn out? Is he hungry? Is he tired? Disillusioned? Faithful? Excited? Imagine the wind blowing through his hair, but not only imagine it, *feel it*. Remember a time in your life when you felt wind on your face and bring that to your meditation. Try to feel what Moses might have felt on top of that mountain, with very little water, alone.

Then imagine the bush. It can be as big or small as you want it. Imagine it starting to burn—slowly, smoldering at first. The smoke fills Moses's nostrils. It fills your nostrils as well. He watches it burn. You watch it burn. He's perplexed at what he is seeing. Even though wildfires are common in this arid region of the world, this bush doesn't seem to be burning into ashes.

Imagine what you would have felt if you were in the desert valley of a mountain. Imagine what you would have felt if the bush started talking to you. How is the bush communicating to you? Through words? Through impressions? Through inspired feelings? Is there an inner voice talking to Moses, or is Moses hearing the thunderous boom of the Almighty? What does the bush say? How would you react?

Take the time to quiet your mind and listen. You may not hear anything. Your mind might again race to something you need to take care of at work or at home. Accept it and then let it go and listen to the scene you are in. What do you hear?

12

The Resurrection: Past, Present, Future

Imagine for a moment a huge, flat-roofed, glass house. It has three floors. On the bottom floor is your past—all the things that have ever happened to you. The second floor is your present, only it's not as crowded as the first floor because your present moment is really fleeting. In some ways, your present is like the middle part of a child's slide in a park. Your future lingers at the top for a moment and then takes off. That middle part of the slide, when you're sliding, that's the present. Before you know it, you land on the bottom and your feet touch the ground in your past.

The present moment is so hard to hold on to, isn't it? I mean, let's try to hold on to the present moment coming up.

Ready.

Set.

Go.

Grab it!

Did you catch it?

Me neither.

So, we have the first two floors. The third floor is your future, and these are all the events in your life that haven't happened yet. The future is constantly changing depending on how you slide through your present moment. Maybe as you're sliding down, you put your feet out and slow down your momentum, or maybe you look to the side and see a friend and wave. Maybe you hiccup. Every little change on the way down affects when the future takes flight.

So, to sum up so far: we have a glass house and it contains all your experiences. Your past. Your present. Your future.

The Glass House Exercise #1:
The Glass Elevator

Let's pretend there's a glass elevator connected to the top of the house and you can ride this elevator up high into the sky. The elevator has a glass floor so you can see down clearly as you lift off.

Look down at your life now.

What do you see?

Let's call this God's viewpoint. Your past, present, and future look as if they are happening simultaneously. There is no sense of time because from this point of view, it's all happening at once. This means that eternity isn't something linear, starting six billion years ago and continuing on six billion years into the future and beyond. Eternity isn't big at all. It's a single point, a still point, as T. S. Eliot said, in space. The farther you fly into the sky, the more difficult it becomes to see any separation in time, to see any separation of bodies or space. Climb even higher and you see that bodies occupy the same space. Eternity isn't something vast. It's a single, glorious, beautiful moment.

Imagine that this is happening for all people. That the glass house itself is vast and there are people who intersect your life at certain spaces. Maybe someone intersects with you in your future, but because time is just a single moment, when you meet that person in the present, it's as if you knew him always. Or maybe a person runs into you in your past and the two of you talked over a cup of coffee that you don't remember because it happened in his past and you're pretty involved with your present. Then this person appears again in your future—which is really just your present when it finally happens—and there's a familiarity that's uncanny. Maybe you kissed this person at a space in your life. Or maybe you shook this person's hand or bummed a cigarette off that person somewhere in your past—or future—and when you met each other in the present it was as if you always knew that person.

So a man, separated from his beloved by geography for months, is actually spending time with her right now. And a Monday night in a bar in August so long ago, when he was gently overwhelmed by how pretty her hand looked and how her arm, long and distant like a horizon, freckled with stars, made him lose his breath, wasn't a single occurrence but a constant happening that continues to unfold right now.

What am I trying to say? That our lives have intersected many times in this single moment in eternity. Which in turn means that Jesus's life, death, and resurrection weren't single occurrences that happened two thousand years ago but are events happening in our lives right now, right here, right in front of you even though you may not be aware of it. Whether we know it or not, we are participating in a single eternal moment.

God is present here. Among and within. Everything you do affects not just the people in your immediate life but the lives of all people, whether it's a neighbor you've never spoken to or an old man with sweaty hands in Beijing.

The Glass Elevator Exercise #2: Shared Space

Imagine for a moment that there are two people standing about ten feet from one another. Oh, and that they are standing beneath a glass elevator. Let's imagine that these two people are mortal enemies. They are each other's arch nemesis. Maybe they're snarling at each other or saying a few choice words, but they are not allowed to move and for this exercise they won't. You, however, will.

Where are you? Well, you're inside the glass elevator and it's crystal clear (before you got in, someone really scrubbed that thing down with vinegar and newspaper). You look down and you see these two below you. They are ten feet away.

You press the button, the motor engages, and you move upward—let's say one story. You look down. The enemies are still there. Still about ten feet away from each other. You press the button again and ascend about four more stories. You look down. There they are, exchanging hand gestures, but something seems a bit different. You can't tell what, but something seems strange.

You move up another fifty feet. You are now one hundred feet high above the two enemies, and it dawns on you what's happening. From this height, it seems that the two enemies are much closer together than when you first saw them.

You rise another nine hundred feet. You are now a thousand feet above them. You know they cannot move, but now with your excellent vision it seems the distance between them has been cut in half. You rise higher, doubling your distance, and now it seems that the two people below you are only inches away from each other. You rise higher, miles over the two people, and they look as if they are maybe an inch away from each other. You burst through the atmosphere as you rise higher into space and the two enemies appear to be sharing the same space.

You continue moving into space, and soon towns and countries all dissolve into a single cell, or a pale blue dot, as Carl Sagan once said.

This is how God sees us: Not as separate. Not as distant from one another, but as members of the body of Christ. You share the same space with seven billion other people. What you do to your neighbor, you do to yourself; what you do to the lesser, Jesus says, you do to me.

Imagine someone you don't like. Someone you detest. Someone you need to forgive. Imagine you are standing across from that person and the glass elevator is equipped with a camera that projects your image and the image of your enemy onto a large TV screen. As the elevator rises, you watch as the distance between you narrows until you occupy the same space.

13

The Hands of God

In our fast-paced, hectic world it is sometimes very easy to let our worries burden us and take control of our lives. When life's problems have become too big, when you've done all you can do and can do no more, it's time to turn them over to a higher power and place them in the hands of God.

The hand of God is a universal symbol, one depicted in art and words over the centuries. We find it in the Thirty-Seventh Psalm, "If the LORD delights in a man's way, he makes his steps firm; though he stumble, he will not fall, for the LORD upholds him with his hand," and in Auguste Rodin's sculpture *The Hand of God*, which depicts the creation of man. From Norman Vincent Peale we read in *The Power of Positive Thinking*: "Put yourself in God's hands. To do that simply state, 'I am in God's hands.' Then believe you are NOW receiving all the power you need. 'Feel' it flowing into you."

In this meditation you will place your problems in the hands of God.

God's Hands Exercise

Imagine before you two outstretched hands. The palms are up and the hands come together as if they are cupping falling water. Hold that image in your mind until it becomes very clear. You can picture the valley these two hands create, and you can see the lines of the palms that look like the contours of a map. These are big hands. These are strong hands. These are powerful hands.

Consider another image. With your eyes still closed, think of a problem in your life, something you've been worrying about but over which you have absolutely no control. Maybe you have a toothache and you've called your dentist but she can't see you until tomorrow afternoon because she's lounging on a beach in Mexico. Maybe you're late on your rent because an important check hasn't cleared for you. Maybe your husband or wife is having a difficult time at work and the horror of layoffs hangs over your heads like a dark cloud. Maybe a dear friend of yours is sick. Whatever it is, picture the problem in your mind. Okay. Got it?

I want you to take that image, that problem, the thing you've been worrying about, and I want you to place it in the open hands we talked about earlier. How do you do that? You can imagine the problem as if it were a snapshot, a photograph, or a still life and imagine yourself laying the problem in the palms of these two humongous hands.

Repeat these words: "I place my problems in the hands of God and have faith that everything will work out the way it is supposed to."

14

The Examen

Several years ago I became a father. My wife and I came to a very important decision after we brought our son home from the hospital. It had nothing to do with his diet or religion or what school he eventually would attend. It had to do with video games.

My wife and I agreed that we would keep our son away from video games for as long as possible. Both of us had spent years in front of a TV playing the likes of *Super Mario Bros.* and *Donkey Kong* and dozens of others. We did not want our children to waste as much time as we did (we each spent a serious amount of time playing when we could have been spending time with our respective families or friends or reading or praying or doing whatever).

We were very good with our first child. Granted, some people thought we were raising him in the Amish tradition because he didn't know what a game controller was, but we were good for four years.

And then . . .

Enter the villain of this story. Our son's aunt Josie.

Josie loves video games.

When my wife was in the hospital delivering our second child, our four-year-old son spent the night with his aunt, who introduced him to Nintendo.

It was over.

All the hard work, all the talking in secret codes for four years—ruined by my sister-in-law.

Over the next few months all I heard was a crying baby and our son whining for me to buy him a Nintendo DS, a hand-held computer game. I refused! No son of mine was going to waste all his time playing video games. (I did feel a bit like St. Augustine, who, after fathering a child and living a lascivious life, converted to Christianity and then said no one could ever do what he did because it was naughty.)

Well, my son kept asking. He kept knocking. Well, I caved.

I ordered my son a Nintendo from Amazon and three days later it arrived in the mail. The moment I saw that box, I knew I had done a bad thing, so I just left the box in the living room as I debated what to do. To give or not to give, that was the question. My son had no idea I had ordered the game for him, and he kept nagging me to buy one for him. *Every day.*

Then something started to happen. I started looking at the box in a way I never expected. My son would pass that box every day, and not once did he ever think to ask, "Hey, what's inside the box?" He would be inches away from it. Sometimes he would run his small hand over the lettering, but at no time did he ever suspect that what he desired, the thing he wanted most in life, was actually already in his presence.

Something took form in me and I felt it rise inside me. That box for me became God. I don't mean it changed shape or started talking to me, and I definitely don't mean it turned into a golden idol that I worshiped. But I saw God in that box.

So many of us have this desire, this yearning to know God, to be with God, to have joy in God, and many of us go on long, arduous journeys to find him. But how many of us ever ask ourselves, *Is God here with me now? Is the God I desire here with me right now? And if he is, how do I react to him?*

These two questions form the basis of the Examen.

The Examen, a core component of St. Ignatius's teaching, involves setting aside time to reflect on the activities and thoughts of the day. In this simple meditation, we ask ourselves primarily two questions: Where was God for me? What was my response to those encounters?

This simple, six-step process is a gentle, and sometimes startling, way of finding God in our daily lives, and it helps us learn from our actions—and reactions. Many of us may talk a good game; we may talk about love for God and neighbor or speak excitedly about the gifts in our lives, but our actions say otherwise. The Examen is a bit like a spiritual chiropractor, helping bring your desires into alignment with God's will—and conversely, it helps bring your will into alignment with God's desire.

Oh, and did I give my son the Nintendo? Of course. I'm a pushover.

Examen Exercise

Many people suggest performing the Examen twice a day, around lunchtime and then again before you go to sleep, but it can be done at any time of the day.

Step 1: Using one of the breathing techniques discussed earlier in this book, attempt to quiet your mind. You might resist, but don't put pressure on yourself to conform to any preconceived notion about what your silence should be. Just allow yourself, like water, to find level.

Step 2: Remind yourself that God is all around you. He's inside you and outside you and his heart beats in all creation.

Step 3: Ask the Holy Spirit to rise up inside you and give you the wisdom to acknowledge God in your life and the gifts that are all around you. Ask the Spirit for guidance in reviewing your actions.

Step 4: Give thanks for the day. Turn your eyes into microscopes and look for God in all things, the good and the bad. Find God in a book you are reading, in music you're listening to, in your loved ones, and in the rude bus driver who's always barking at you, in the annoying coworker with the staring problem, and in the electric bill that arrives in the mail. Finding God in a flower can be easy. Finding God in some jerk who cuts you off in traffic . . . well, there's the rub.

Step 5: Take inventory of your day. Ask questions and give honest answers.

Where was God for you today?

- Was God walking with you, or did you ignore him the way a child ignores a friend he's grown tired of?
- Was God present in your actions?
- Was he present in your thoughts?
- If God was giving you the silent treatment, was it God who was being difficult, or were you wearing earplugs?
- Did you show love to people?

- Were you rude, or did you treat a person unfairly?
- Did you really have to send that e-mail?
- Were you trying to get one over on a coworker?
- Did you show love to the people in your life?
- Did you show love to strangers?

Step 6: With the help of the Holy Spirit, make it a priority to reconcile your actions. If you feel you failed, ask God for guidance, strength, and forgiveness. And if you did a good job, well, be excited and build on that gift.

15

Dying to God

I died one night, some years ago, on a fog-entrenched medieval bridge in an Eastern European city.

When I was in my mid-twenties, a few years out of college, I had this harebrained, Ralph Kramden-like scheme to change my life. I was going to live mythically. What exactly did I mean by that? I wanted to imitate the life of Jesus. The first way I was going to do that was to spend forty days and forty nights in the desert. Now, I'm pretty fair-skinned and I burn rather easily in the sun—plus, the heat makes me feel really uncomfortable—so I decided to substitute the streets of Europe for the arid, sun-scorched sands of a barren wilderness. I would much prefer coffee and chocolate pastries than a diet of morning dew and locusts.

Seriously convinced that this was the right thing to do, and with very little money in my pocket (not to mention a bank account filled not with greenbacks but with cobwebs), I quit my job and set off to work out my salvation. (I was in my twenties at the time, so cut me some slack!)

In the middle of this journey I found myself standing on the blackened, cobblestoned walkway of the Charles Bridge, in Prague—a seven-hundred-year-old construction adorned with life-size statues of Jesus and the saints. I was with my friend Anna, who was living in the city at the time. It was a cool night in October. There was a full moon, and a fog was circling around everything like a lazy, fat cat that wanted to go to sleep.

We were not alone. The bridge, a central artery that connected the old Prague with the new Prague, was a magnet for tourists, street artists, lovers, and the lost. Many of us that night had formed a loose circle around two musicians—a guitarist and a violinist, who were playing a Rachmaninoff piece—when a well-dressed man with designer clothes, long brown hair, and a beard bisected the crowd and stood before us staring at the moon.

"Look," I said to my friend, "it's Jesus."

"Yes," she said. "Resurrection has been good to him."

We both smiled, and as I watched this man, who seemed entranced by the moon and the music and the night, something began to change inside me. I felt surprised and unsettled, as if I had been given a gift I wasn't expecting. Time seemed to perform a slow somersault, and a few words of the joke I'd voiced only a moment ago began to awe and frighten me. My eyes darted around the bridge. Chills seemed less to come from within me as much as to be pressed upon me.

I was looking at the face of Christ.

Not just this rich man in Gucci and Armani, but the musicians, the beggars, the lovers holding hands, the students, the children, all these strangers—all these people I would never see again—seemed to remove the mask of their temporal existence, and beneath all these exposed faces was the visage of Christ. Then the words of Paul came flooding into my mind:

> For just as the body is one and has many members, and all the members of the body, though many, are one body, so it is with Christ. For in the one Spirit we were all baptized into one body—Jews or Greeks, slaves or free—and we were all made to drink of one Spirit. Indeed, the body does not consist of one member but of many. . . . Now you are the body of Christ and individually members of it. (1 Corinthians 12:12–14, 27)

I died that night and have never been the same again.

Anyone who sees God's face will die.

I remember these words from my early days in Catholic school.

> Moses said, "Show me your glory, I pray." And he said, "I will make all my goodness pass before you, and will proclaim before you the name, 'The LORD'; and I will be gracious to whom I will be gracious, and will show mercy on whom I will show mercy. But," he said, "you cannot see my face; for no one shall see me and live." (Exodus 33:18–20)

Some teachers love to scare the God out of us, and those words certainly did the trick for me, so much so that I would pray at night never to see the face of God.

"Ask and it will be given to you." Well, I asked and God gave me what I wanted: spiritual blindness.

For years I would just look at people as people. I never saw God in anything. God was distant. God was frightening. God was like Medusa. Look upon him and you would turn to stone.

Yet after that spiritual—and very real—death in Prague, I was resurrected in a profound and simple way. I had been transformed and began to see God in all things—not only in the people I passed in the street, my family, my friends, and even my enemies, but also in the land I walked on, the buildings I stood beneath, the bread I ate, the wine I drank, even the plastic I threw away in a garbage can. Certainly, if we are created in God's image, then the face of my neighbor is the face of God. If Christ is God fully present in human form, then the face of a one-legged, toothless beggar staring back at me on a city street is the face of Christ asking for help.

We are, as Paul says in 1 Corinthians 6, the temple of the Holy Spirit. In turn, each of us is an ark of the covenant, the chest that held the Ten Commandments, only this time we contain within us the Word of God, Jesus, who is present in us through the power of the Holy Person, otherwise known as the Holy Spirit. To look at others and see God within them is a gift for us.

Yet this gift is an uncomfortable one, one in fact that shames me, because more often than not I turn away from God's face. I don't want to die to my old ways. No matter how many people like to romanticize dying in poetry, literature, and theology, dying sucks. It's painful and frightening. Dying to God is no less than that.

Yet when I have allowed the Holy Spirit to flow courage through my soul—when I've stopped acting like a closed-eyed child walking through a haunted house on Halloween night—and actually looked upon the face of God, it was the most beautiful of all experiences. In that death is the seed of resurrection—a new life—one in which, if only for a moment, you remove your own mask and expose, if ever so briefly, the Christ within you who yearns to show his face.

Dying to God Exercise

Imagine for a moment that you are standing a hundred feet away from a painting of the face of Jesus. It doesn't matter what that face looks like. It could be a famous work of art, an image from a movie, a child's crayon drawing—whatever makes you feel most comfortable. Now, recite the Jesus Prayer and take a step toward that image. Repeat the prayer and take another step. You're getting closer to the painting. What may have looked like something the size of a stamp from that initial distance is starting to grow in size.

As you repeat the prayer, move closer to the painting. As you do, you begin to notice the painting isn't a painting at all. It's a mosaic, and the closer you get, the more you realize that this mosaic is made up of tiny images of people whose lives have intersected your own. There are photos of people in your family, of friends, strangers, coworkers, and people you don't remember but whom you passed in the streets or on the highway. There is the waitress from the diner you visited when you were ten and the teacher you had a crush on, whose name you've long forgotten.

As you move closer, the images become bigger and bigger and you begin to notice that the photos making up this mosaic are in fact also mosaics themselves, and within those are more images of people who have crossed their lives with yours. Continue moving closer to the image, repeating the Jesus Prayer, and keep your eyes and mind open for Jesus. He's in there waiting for you to notice.

16

Thanksgiving

It is very easy to take our world, our loved ones, ourselves, and our God for granted. Every morning when we wake up, then throughout the day, and before we go to sleep, we should take a few moments to give thanks. But *not too much thanks*, as the following story demonstrates.

The setting is an office in New York City. A confused, disorganized young man is trying to collate a number of different reports. Enter a levelheaded young woman who gives the young man a paper clip. He looks at her, and he looks at the clip. For a moment he's speechless. Smiling, he shuffles his papers around and slips on the clip. There is a sigh of relief and then the lights dim and a spotlight shines on the young man, who turns to a nonexistent audience and begins to speak.

"Oh my. Wow. I can't even believe this. This is such an honor. This paper clip changed my life and I just want to say thanks to a few people for making this happen.

"First off, I would like to thank my coworker Darya, who gave me this paper clip. If it weren't for her kindness and generosity, I wouldn't be standing here today.

"I would like to thank Pete in the mail room. Pete is the guy who brings the supplies we order to our offices. He's always friendly, and Pete, I know you're working two jobs to support your family, and I want to say thank you just for bringing Darya that box of paper clips. I want to thank your family too for the sacrifices they have to make because you work so much. They know you love them.

"I would like to thank the paper supply company that shipped those clips to our office. Thank you just for having a business that keeps us from losing our minds. Thank you not only to the heads of the company but to all your employees who are the backbone of the corporation.

"I would like to thank the UPS guy who makes deliveries to our office every day. I would also like to thank your parents, man, for bringing you into the world. Thank you.

"I would like to thank the manufacturers of the cardboard that created the box that holds the paper clips and all those workers in your plant who show up for work every day, in desperate need of caffeine, but ready to work. Thank you to all their families as well, including all sons and daughters who might be getting married and starting families of their own soon.

"A special shout-out to the people who make the ink that's printed on the cardboard box and the designer who designed the logo. You guys never get the credit you deserve. Keep on rocking.

"Thank you to the truck drivers who move the supplies for the warehouse to the stores, and thanks to all the civil engineers who helped design all the roads that we all drive on every day, and the municipal workers who keep the roads *relatively* clean and safe (I just ran over a pothole the other day). Oh, and thank you to those folks who create the traffic lights that prevent chaos in our nation.

"Thank you to all the people who fed and clothed all these people.

"I would also like to thank the inventors of the paper clip, including Samuel B. Fay, Erlman J. Wright, and all the folks at Britain's Gem Manufacturing Company who worked back in the 1890s to get clips out to the world. And a special thanks to Johan Vaaler of Norway. I know it's been proved that Johan is not the originator of the paper clip, but without him we wouldn't have all the folklore and legend surrounding this little bit of metal. And we definitely wouldn't have that giant sculpture of a paper clip outside the Norwegian School of Management in Sandvika, Norway.

"I know these paper clips are manufactured in China, which is wild, right? How many thousands of miles need to be traversed to get those clips from overseas? It's unfathomable to me. Anyway, I would like to thank all the folks in China who work in the factories that produce these clips as well as the drivers and all the dockworkers on both sides of the world who were involved in getting the clips from the factory to the ports.

"Thank you to all the people who mined the metal for these clips, and thank you to all the animals and plants that were displaced during this time so I could hold my paper together.

"And last, I want to thank God, who has been involved in this project from its inception and was in all the people and things that helped along the way. We are all connected and we do live in abundance even if we sometimes feel disconnected and empty. Thank you, God. Thank you. Thank you. Thank you!"

∞

This is why it's not good to be too thankful. If you were, you'd never get out of bed, and you'd probably never get any work done. So use common sense when giving thanks, but make sure you do it every day.

The Acceptance Speech Exercise: Did You See God Today?

When you wake up in the morning or right before you go to sleep, take a few moments to give thanks to God, the people, and the things in your life by tracing how each intersects with your existence. Of course, people are more important than things, but each thing is infused with the life of the people who assisted in creating it. Each person, in turn, is infused with God the Creator.

Then ask yourself this question: *Did I notice God in that person and thing today?* If the answer is no, ask yourself why and then ask the Holy Spirit for guidance in your search.

17

The Geometry of the Cross

Picture for a moment a simple cross. You can even draw one if that helps. Here, I'll do it for you.

As you can see, I have the artistic skills of someone who has just discovered crayons for the first time. Even though it's a bit shaky and uneven, I have to say that's a pretty good-looking cross. Aside from those who see it as a lowercase *t*, you'll notice what it is right away. A cross, after all, is a very simple draw-ing. It is really just two lines that run over each other.

I hate to do this to you, but I would like to talk briefly about math—geometry, to be more specific. I promise this will take only a few moments.

One of the most basic ideas in geometry is that when two lines intersect, they do so at a single point. Let's look at the picture of the cross again, only this time I want you to think of the line moving from the bottom to the top as God, and then I want you to consider the line moving from left to right as humanity.

You will see that these two lines meet at a specific point in space. Let's call that point *Jesus.*

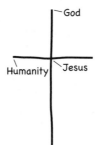

Here we have the line of eternity, the timeless, the infinite God, intersecting with the line of the time-bound, the temporal, the finite person. Spirit crossing flesh, coming together at one point in time and space—Jesus, the infinite man.

Let's consider that the line of God includes all his creation: birds, mountains, rivers, shopping malls, barracks, your family, strangers, even rude people on cell phones or behind the wheels of an endless array of SUVs in grocery-store parking lots. Let's also consider that the person in question is you.

Examining this new information, we will see that whenever or wherever we encounter God's creation, no matter how beautiful or how ugly, no matter how loving or how annoying, we intersect at one point, and that point is Jesus. Where we find God's creation—all his creation—we will also find Jesus. No matter where you turn or what you do, he is there, in front of you, behind you, cooing at you from behind the eyes of a newborn baby or barking at you from behind the counter at the Department of Motor Vehicles.

"This is all fine and well," you may be saying, "but I am also part of God's creation, so shouldn't I be included on the line that runs from bottom to top?" Well, yes, that is a very good point (or in this case, line). You will notice that when we do this, when we include you not only on the line that moves from left to right, but also bottom to top, when you encounter yourself—whether it be the face looking back at you in the mirror or the reflection of your soul against God's creation—you will find Jesus:

- Where did you meet God today on your road to life?
- Breathe in the Our Father and meditate on the times you were aware that your life intersected with God.

18

Editing

Some years back, while fighting a bad case of insomnia, I switched on the TV and caught the tail end of a documentary about DVDs. In it, legendary film director Martin Scorsese talked about the importance of watching movies in widescreen as compared to full-screen formats. What's the difference? Well, Scorsese said that when you watch movies on TV, normally you would see a disclaimer at the very beginning that said something like this: "This movie has been formatted to fit your screen." Since most people at the time of the documentary owned TVs that looked like boxes, this meant that a film shown in 35mm (which has a rectangular shape) in the movie theater, when shown on TV, literally had its left and right sides cut off. On average, you were seeing only seventy percent of what the director had originally intended you to see.

If memory serves me here, I believe Scorsese went on to show a scene from *The Sound of Music* starring Julie Andrews. It was the opening scene when she twirls around in the Austrian Alps. Shown next to a clip that had been edited to fit the TV screen, you could definitely see a difference. In widescreen you watched the artist's intended vision. In TV full format, you missed out on some beautiful, intentional images that were essential to the viewer's experience.

He also compared movie and TV versions of scenes from his movie *Taxi Driver*; in the TV format, during one pivotal sequence, you could see only Robert De Niro up against a wall. In widescreen, you saw the character against the wall, but you also saw the cops on the other side of the wall closing in on him.

This may have been just a well-done commercial to sell widescreen DVDs, but I don't think so. Scorsese talked with such passion about the disservice that full format had done to movies, the actors, and directors, and to the viewers who watched them. Well, he had me sold, and from then on I watched every movie I could in widescreen. Certainly, you had these black abysses on the top and bottom of the screen, but you could watch the full picture, the full intention of the director.

The more I watched, the more I saw that Scorsese hadn't just been talking about movies; he had been talking about life as well. I had been doing a disservice to God's artistry. I began to see that spiritually, I had cut off the ends of my experience. I could see in front of me, but that was it. I had spiritual myopia and was missing the beauty on the sides. How many people had I passed on the street because all I did was see directly in front of me? How many people had I not helped? How many trees or facades had I walked past in my life?

Spiritual exercises—daily commitment to prayer and meditation—help us see in widescreen, help us see the panorama of God's creation, and help us see that, during those times when we think *God's not present in my full-format world*, all we need to do is pray. As the screen of my vision expands, I see that God was standing there all along, in the film of my life—I had just cut out the side he was standing on.

Scorsese Exercise

Close your eyes. Repeat the Jesus Prayer until you come to a relaxing place of quiet. In the darkness of your closed eyes, begin to roll film. Imagine that you are experiencing something important in your life. Maybe it's your first date, your graduation, or the birth of your child. Create specific images in your mind. Try to expand your vision and see that experience in widescreen and imagine that God is there in the scene with you now, standing to the side, but in the event. He was there all along, but those stupid TVs. . . .

Part Four: Exercising with the Parables

A question was proposed to a group: if God were a tree, what kind of tree would he be?

The people thought about this, and after a few minutes of reflection, they began to speak, one at a time.

"God is a huge oak tree because God is strong and his roots are deep."

"God is a sycamore because I used to pray under one of those trees when I was a child."

"God is an elm tree because he gives me shade and because, well, I like elm trees."

"God is a weeping willow tree because the weeping willow is the most magnificent tree I've ever seen. There is one by a monastery near my home. On weekends in autumn, in the moments between night and dawn, I will walk to that field and enter under its canopy. I sit there on one of the long arms close to the ground and listen to the geese fly overhead."

"I'm from Arizona and there aren't many trees where I live. God is a cactus."

"In a book called *The Little Prince* there's a tree that's an entire world, and the Little Prince visits it. I always thought that was a beautiful image, a single giant tree on a tiny planet. Maybe that planet is heaven and all the angels live in its branches."

"I don't really like trees—all the leaves you have to clean up in the fall. God's not a tree to me."

"I know someone said that the weeping willow is the most magnificent tree in the world, but I'm assuming that's only because he's never seen a redwood. I was in that forest some years back, and you'd be amazed at the size of these trees. I mean, they're as big as this room and some of them have been around for thousands of years. They stretch so high into the sky that you can't see where they end. That is God to me."

Jesus was sitting in the room at the time, though no one recognized him. When it was his turn to speak, he said, "God for me is like the Charlie Brown Christmas tree."

"You mean that skinny little thing from the cartoon?" asked someone.

"Yes. For me, God is fragile and naked, and most people pass him by without giving him much thought. The only people who seem to know the beauty that lies within are children who don't know any better."

"Good grief," moaned someone eating grapes.

19

The Parable of the Sower (Day 1)

What follows is a seven-day spiritual exercise plan to illuminate the parables of Christ by incorporating variations of the Jesus Prayer, centering prayer, and lectio divina. *Each day includes basic exercises, a reading from the Gospels, and questions for reflection.*

- Begin with an Our Father. When you have completed the prayer, focus your attention on the first word: *our*. Try not to think about it, but let it sit with you. What does it make you feel? How does that feeling relate to your life?

- Say the Jesus Prayer while consciously breathing in and out.

- Breathe in: "Lord Jesus Christ."

- Breathe out: "Have mercy on me."

- Repeat this prayer until you feel rested and focused, and then move on to the day's reading.

That same day Jesus went out of the house and sat beside the lake. Such great crowds gathered around him that he got into a boat and sat there, while the whole crowd stood on the beach. And he told them many things in parables, saying: "Listen! A sower went out to sow. And as he sowed, some seeds fell on the path, and the birds came and ate them up. Other seeds fell on rocky ground, where they did not have much soil, and they sprang up quickly, since they had no depth of soil. But when the sun rose, they were scorched; and since they had no root, they withered away. Other seeds fell among thorns, and the thorns grew up and choked them. Other seeds fell on good soil and brought forth grain, some a hundredfold, some sixty, some thirty. Let anyone with ears listen!" Then the disciples came and asked him, "Why do you speak to them in parables?" (Matthew 13:1–10)

- What word stood out for you in the reading? Focus on that word and let it be with you. Repeat it and ask God for help in understanding why that word struck a chord with you.
- Who is the sower? What are the seeds?
- Where in your life do you find healthy soil?
- How can you become healthy soil?

20

The Parable of the Greatest in the Kingdom of Heaven (Day 2)

- Begin by saying the Our Father. When you are done, focus on the word *father*. Let the word sit with you. What does *father* mean to you? Is your image of *father* one of comfort? If not, how does your relationship with your earthly father affect the way you imagine God the Father to be?
- Repeat the Prayer of the Sacred Heart while consciously focusing on your breath.
- Breathe in: "Sacred heart of Jesus."
- Breathe out: "I trust in thee."
- Repeat this until you feel relaxed and comforted and then move on to the day's reading.

At that time the disciples came to Jesus and asked, "Who is the greatest in the kingdom of heaven?" He called a child, whom he put among them, and said, "Truly I tell you, unless you change and become like children, you will never enter the kingdom of heaven. Whoever becomes humble like this child is the greatest in the kingdom of heaven." (Matthew 18:1–4)

- What word stood out for you in the reading? Focus on that word and let it be with you. Repeat it and ask God for help in understanding why that word struck a chord with you.

21

The Parable of the Lost Sheep (Day 3)

- Begin by saying the Our Father. When you have completed the prayer, focus on the word *who*. Who is God to you? Who is the Holy Spirit? Who is Christ? Meditate on Jesus's words: "Who do you say I am?" Who are you?

- Repeat "Come, Holy Spirit, come." Breathe the words in and out. Feel the Holy Spirit rising inside you. Feel the power of God coursing through your body and soul. Then move on to your reading.

Take care that you do not despise one of these little ones; for, I tell you, in heaven their angels continually see the face of my Father in heaven. What do you think? If a shepherd has a hundred sheep, and one of them has gone astray, does he not leave the ninety-nine on the mountains and go in search of the one that went astray? And if he finds it, truly I tell you, he rejoices over it more than over the ninety-nine that never went astray. So it is not the will of your Father in heaven that one of these little ones should be lost. (Matthew 18:10–14)

- If we are all God's children, aren't we all "little ones"? If so, have you ever looked down on God's little ones? Why?
- Have you ever lost something and tried desperately to find it? Do you ever feel lost? Why?
- Do you believe God is searching for you? Ask God to help you be found.

22

The Parable of the Unmerciful Servant (Day 4)

- Begin with an Our Father. When you have completed the prayer, focus your attention on the word *art*, or the words *to be*. Try not to think about it, but let it sit with you. Who is God to you? Where can he be found?
- Say the Jesus Prayer while consciously breathing in and out.
- Breathe in: "Lord Jesus Christ."
- Breathe out: "Have mercy on me."
- Repeat this prayer until you feel rested and focused and then move on to the day's reading.

Then Peter came and said to him, "Lord, if another member of the church sins against me, how often should I

151

forgive? As many as seven times?" Jesus said to him, "Not seven times, but, I tell you, seventy-seven times."

For this reason the kingdom of heaven may be compared to a king who wished to settle accounts with his slaves. When he began the reckoning, one who owed him ten thousand talents was brought to him; and, as he could not pay, his lord ordered him to be sold, together with his wife and children and all his possessions, and payment to be made. So the slave fell on his knees before him, saying, "Have patience with me, and I will pay you everything." And out of pity for him, the lord of that slave released him and forgave him the debt. But that same slave, as he went out, came upon one of his fellow-slaves who owed him a hundred denarii; and seizing him by the throat, he said, "Pay what you owe." Then his fellow slave fell down and pleaded with him, "Have patience with me, and I will pay you." But he refused; then he went and threw him into prison until he should pay the debt. When his fellow-slaves saw what had happened, they were greatly distressed, and they went and reported to their lord all that had taken place. Then his lord summoned him and said to him, "You wicked slave! I forgave you all that debt because you pleaded with me. Should you not have had mercy on your fellow-slave, as I had mercy on you?" And in anger his lord handed him over to be tortured until he should pay his entire debt. So my heavenly Father will also do to every one of you, if you do not forgive your brother or sister from your heart. (Matthew 18:21–35)

- Focus on the line from the Our Father, "Forgive us our trespasses." Do you practice forgiveness? If so, how? Is there someone in your life you haven't forgiven?
- Are you in need of forgiveness? Ask God for forgiveness and for the strength to forgive others . . . and yourself.

23

The Parable of the Good Samaritan (Day 5)

- Begin by saying the Our Father. When you are done, focus on the words *in heaven*. Let the words sit with you. What is your vision of heaven? How do you feel being a part of a community of saints and angels? What do you see when you picture heaven?
- Repeat the Prayer of the Sacred Heart while consciously focusing on your breath.
- Breathe in: "Sacred heart of Jesus."
- Breathe out: "I trust in thee."
- Repeat this until you feel relaxed and comforted and then move on to the day's reading.

Just then a lawyer stood up to test Jesus. "Teacher," he said, "what must I do to inherit eternal life?" He said to him,

"What is written in the law? What do you read there?" He answered, "You shall love the Lord your God with all your heart, and with all your soul, and with all your strength, and with all your mind; and your neighbor as yourself." And he said to him, "You have given the right answer; do this, and you will live."

But wanting to justify himself, he asked Jesus, "And who is my neighbor?" Jesus replied, "A man was going down from Jerusalem to Jericho, and fell into the hands of robbers, who stripped him, beat him, and went away, leaving him half dead. Now by chance a priest was going down that road; and when he saw him, he passed by on the other side. So likewise a Levite, when he came to the place and saw him, passed by on the other side. But a Samaritan while travelling came near him; and when he saw him, he was moved with pity. He went to him and bandaged his wounds, having poured oil and wine on them. Then he put him on his own animal, brought him to an inn, and took care of him. The next day he took out two denarii, gave them to the innkeeper, and said, 'Take care of him; and when I come back, I will repay you whatever more you spend.' Which of these three, do you think, was a neighbor to the man who fell into the hands of the robbers?" He said, "The one who showed him mercy." Jesus said to him, "Go and do likewise." (Luke 10:25–37)

- When have you shown mercy to others? Who has shown mercy to you?

- How can you show mercy, not just to your family and friends, but to strangers as well? How can you "go and do likewise"?

24

The Parable of the Workers in the Vineyard (Day 6)

- Begin by saying the Our Father. When you have completed the prayer, focus on the words *hallowed be thy name*. What does hallowed mean to you? What is the importance of God's name? How can you keep God's name holy in your life?

- Repeat "Come, Holy Spirit, come." Breathe the words in and out of you. Feel the Holy Spirit rising inside you. Feel the power of God coursing through your body and soul, and then move on to your reading.

For the kingdom of heaven is like a landowner who went out early in the morning to hire laborers for his vineyard. After agreeing with the laborers for the usual daily wage, he sent them into his vineyard. When he went out about nine o'clock, he saw others standing idle in the market-place; and he said to them, "You also go into the vineyard, and I will pay you whatever is right." So they went. When he went out again about noon and about three o'clock, he did the same. And about five o'clock he went out and found others standing around; and he said to them, "Why are you standing here idle all day?" They said to him, "Because no one has hired us." He said to them, "You also go into the vineyard." When evening came, the owner of the vineyard said to his manager, "Call the laborers and give them their pay, beginning with the last and then going to the first." When those hired about five o'clock came, each of them received the usual daily wage. Now when the first came, they thought they would receive more; but each of them also received the usual daily wage. And when they received it, they grumbled against the landowner, saying, "These last worked only one hour, and you have made them equal to us who have borne the burden of the day and the scorching heat." But he replied to one of them, "Friend, I am doing you no wrong; did you not agree with me for the usual daily wage? Take what belongs to you and go; I choose to give to this last the same as I give to you. Am I not allowed to do what I choose with what belongs to me? Or are you envious because I am generous?" So the last will be first, and the first will be last. (Matthew 20:1–16)

- Do you live in an abundant world?

- Do you sometimes get angry at God's generosity to others? Do you ever feel slighted by God?
- How can you emulate the generosity of God in your life?

25

The Parable of the Lost Son (Day 7)

- Begin with an Our Father. When you have completed the prayer, focus your attention on the words *Thy kingdom come, thy will be done, on earth as it is in heaven. Thy will be done:* what do these words mean to you? What does the phrase *thy kingdom come* mean to you? How can you surrender to God's will in your day-to-day life? And what does the mysterious phrase, *on earth as it is in heaven*, say about the nature of reality? Say the Jesus Prayer while consciously breathing in and out.
- Breathe in: "Lord Jesus Christ,"
- Breathe out: "Have mercy on me."
- Repeat this prayer until you feel rested and focused and then move on to the day's reading.

Then Jesus said, "There was a man who had two sons. The younger of them said to his father, 'Father, give me the share of the property that will belong to me.' So he divided his property between them. A few days later the younger son gathered all he had and travelled to a distant country, and there he squandered his property in dissolute living. When he had spent everything, a severe famine took place throughout that country, and he began to be in need. So he went and hired himself out to one of the citizens of that country, who sent him to his fields to feed the pigs. He would gladly have filled himself with the pods that the pigs were eating; and no one gave him anything. But when he came to himself he said, "How many of my father's hired hands have bread enough and to spare, but here I am dying of hunger! I will get up and go to my father, and I will say to him, 'Father, I have sinned against heaven and before you; I am no longer worthy to be called your son; treat me like one of your hired hands.'" So he set off and went to his father. But while he was still far off, his father saw him and was filled with compassion; he ran and put his arms around him and kissed him. Then the son said to him, 'Father, I have sinned against heaven and before you; I am no longer worthy to be called your son.' But the father said to his slaves, 'Quickly, bring out a robe—the best one—and put it on him; put a ring on his finger and sandals on his feet. And get the fatted calf and kill it, and let us eat and celebrate; for this son of mine was dead and is alive again; he was lost and is found!' And they began to celebrate.

"Now his elder son was in the field; and when he came and approached the house, he heard music and dancing. He called one of the slaves and asked what was going on. He replied, "Your brother has come, and your father has killed the fatted calf, because he has got him back safe and sound." Then he became angry and refused to go in. His father came out and began to plead with him. But he answered his father, "Listen! For all these years I have been working like a slave for you, and I have never disobeyed your command; yet you have never given me even a young goat so that I might celebrate with my friends. But when this son of yours came back, who has devoured your property with prostitutes, you killed the fatted calf for him!" Then the father said to him, "Son, you are always with me, and all that is mine is yours. But we had to celebrate and rejoice, because this brother of yours was dead and has come to life; he was lost and has been found." (Luke 15:11–32)

- Which character in this story do you relate to the most: The lost son? The older brother? The father?
- Is this story fair? Have you ever felt like the older brother in this story, seemingly penalized or loved less because you have done the right thing while someone else goes off and does wrong?
- How can you reconcile this story with your life?

This completes a week's worth of reflections. For Day 8 and beyond, pick a favorite passage from the Bible and begin your prayer with an Our Father and then, over the course of a week, focus on the remaining words of the prayer: *give us this day / our daily bread / and forgive us our trespasses / as we forgive those who trespass against us / and lead us not into temptation, / but deliver us from evil. / Amen.*

Coda

Some years back, I was walking on a narrow cobblestone street off the Saint-Germaine in Paris when I noticed a scruffy-looking individual kneeling in front of a café. He seemed to be praying, or begging inventively. He appeared to be in his forties and was dressed in black pants and a white shirt. His beard was unkempt, but his hair, which was thinning on top, was handsomely combed. His eyes were closed tight. He rocked gently back and forth, hands clasped in front of him.

I remember that it was late in the afternoon, and the city streets and cafés were beginning to fill with tourists and crepuscular light. No one seemed to be paying this man any attention, and I certainly wasn't going to. But all my life I have been a magnet for misfits, madmen, and mendicants, and just as I was about to turn away my gaze, he opened his eyes, stared right at me, winked, and gave me an I'm-going-to-ask-you-for-money smile. He jumped to his feet with the athleticism of a young man, said something to me in French, and genuflected before me.

"I'm sorry, I don't speak French," I said.

"Ah, Americaaan." He stood up quickly and put out his hand. I shook it. Calloused and strong. "Yes," I said.

"Me!" Slapping his chest, he said, "I lived in Brooklyn for seven years with my brother until he died."

When he said the word *died*, he clasped his hands, raised them to heaven, and said something again in French.

"I'm sorry," I said.

"What is your name?" he asked. His accent was French, and his English was perfect.

I told him.

"Allow me to introduce myself. I am the Re-Brainer." He bowed again to expose the large bald spot on the crown of his head. There was a scab in the center.

"Re-Brainer?"

"Yes, I am the Re-Brainer because I am rethinking the world into a new existence." He pointed to his head. "With my brain!"

"Is that how you hurt yourself?" I pointed to the drying wound.

"Ah," he said, stroking the side of his head. "Sometimes the spirit is so powerful I fall down!"

"What spirit are you talking about?"

He stuck out his chest, placed one hand on his heart, and raised his other high, pointing to the darkening sky. "I have not had a drink since my brother died seven years ago! I am talking about the Holy Spirit! The Holy Spirit! The Spirit that flows through you and me!"

I apologized to him and tried to walk around him.

"Do you pray?" he asked.

"I do."

"I pray all the time! When I am walking, when I am thinking, when I am eating, when I am sleeping, when I am falling." He took a step closer to me, looked over his shoulder, and whispered in my face, "I am praying right now."

He may not have drunk, but he certainly smelled like cigarettes and was in need of a bath.

"Re-Brainer," I said, gently slapping him on the chest, "I rename you Brother Lawrence!"

"Brother Lawrence?"

"Yes, he was a monk who turned his life into a perpetual prayer. Everything he did he believed was a prayer. If he washed a dish, he offered that moment up to God."

He raised both arms in the air, and his smile seemed to eclipse his face. He was missing two teeth. "I am Brother Lawrence, the Re-Brainer! I am rethinking the world into existence! With my brain!"

I had not wanted to talk to the man when he first locked onto me, but now I had to admit, I was intrigued. Nonetheless, I checked my wallet in my pocket and asked him a question. "How are you going to do that, Brother Lawrence, the Re-Brainer?"

"By praying!" He jumped up and down and started to dance in place.

"And your prayers are going to change the world?"

"They already have."

We talked for a few more minutes. About Brooklyn and Coney Island, about his brother, a janitor who died from cancer. About love, booze, cigarettes, Christ, the Virgin Mary, but mostly about the Holy Spirit.

I had grown quickly fond of the man, but it was getting late and I was about to leave and walk on into the growing night.

"Can I have your cigarettes in your pocket?" he asked.

"Sure." I gave him the pack. Brown-papered Nat Shermans from the old store on Forty-Second Street in New York City. I don't smoke anymore.

"I have something for you," he said.

"What is that, Brother Lawrence, the Re-Brainer?"

"It is this." He bent down, and when my eyes followed, I saw that on the ground was an artist's paintbrush. He put it in my hand. His eyes narrowed, and while I don't remember exactly what he said, he whispered a story that went something like this . . .

"This looks like an ordinary paintbrush anyone could buy, but this particular brush has a long and colorful history, of which you are now a part. Originally bought in Cleveland, Ohio, by a mother for her twenty-two-year-old son with dreams of being a world-renowned artist, the brush traveled in the young man's valise, first on a Greyhound bus from Lake Erie Downtown Station to New York City. From there, Henri (for this was the young man's name) departed for Paris, flying nonstop from JFK to Charles de Gaulle airport. It was while studying under the auspices of the International Council for the Preservation of the Humanities that the young man met Antoine, a young vine grower from the Loire Valley with the uncanny ability of changing wine into water.

"Miracle? You may think so. 'A curse,' he called it. They became friends and drank Evian out of burgundy bottles on the banks of the Seine while pontificating on the role of the artist in society (or the lack of role of the artist in present-day society). It was during a night of drunken tomfoolery that the young man's favorite paintbrush, which he always carried with him in the breast pocket of an old coat his father used to wear, was lost during a scuffle with some local boys from the Nord.

"Lying in the street for days, the brush was picked up eventually by a vagrant street magician known in the cafés along the Saint-Germaine as Revoltaire. He used the brush as a disappointing substitute for the Magic Wand of Havana, a gift from his illusionist stepbrother in Cuba, to perform his bits of sleight of hand and chicanery. While trying unsuccessfully to turn a belt into a spotted snake for a group of college students from Australia, this 'Street Christ' (as he was called by his one friend, Father Marcel of Notre Dame de Déception) lost his patience and threw the brush back into the street where it was picked up eventually by a monkey named Pascal.

"Pascal's master, a one-handed accordionist and displaced Irishman named McGreevy, used the paintbrush on occasion as a conductor's baton when he whistled the melody of Edith Piaf's '*Effet que tu me fais*' (the only Piaf song he knew by heart) while Pascal danced his primitive ballet in the streets of the Latin Quarter for loose francs (this was before the currency switched to Euros). One night, as McGreevy and Pascal were walking home (home was a small studio above a chicken house in Montmartre), the brush fell out of a plastic bag and rolled down the long, steep stairs photographed by countless romantics and known as the Stairway of Lovers, near Sacre Coeur. Having traveled nearly one hundred and fifty steps, the brush at full velocity hit a high bump in a cobblestone street and landed in a crate of blank videotapes that were being loaded onto a truck, which was heading to the south of France for the Cannes Film Festival.

"Once the brush made it to the Riviera, it traveled through parts of Switzerland and Italy, carried for a time by the Seven Wandering Jews of Bratislava who had made a wrong turn in Slovakia. Then it changed hands from a pastry chef to a beautiful schoolteacher named Maman to a young crippled violinist named Sophie to an old olive farmer in Sicily named Leo. From there it passed through several more hands—many with arthritis, moles, dry skin, broken fingernails, and gaudy gold rings—and landed in North Africa, where it fell into the possession of a group of Bedouins who mixed cactus wine with the dust of ancient pulverized stars and used the brush to paint astrological charts on the skins of dead camels.

"Unfortunately—for these creations were reported to be the work of the great, great, great, great, great, great, great, great, great, great, great-grandson of one of the Magi who visited Christ at his birth—the brush was stolen by a Gypsy bandit as the Bedouins were trading their desert finds at an oasis for cans of sardines and chickpeas. It did, however, soon find its way to me. What transpired between myself and the Gypsy bandit, I cannot tell you, but you see now that we are all connected, by life, by death, by this brush. I am giving it to you. It is yours and it beckons you to paint!"

I stood with my mouth open, and if it had been a hot midsummer night, not a cool April evening, I'm sure a fly would have flown down my throat. "I'm speechless. I don't know what to say."

"Say nothing," he said. "Paint!"

"I can't paint. I'm a writer."

"You will paint my story with words then."

"No one would believe it."

"Then paint words about prayer," he said.

I looked at the brush and at the eyes of this enflamed soul.

"I promise," I said.

"I am Brother Lawrence," he said, dancing. "The Re-Brainer. I am rethinking the world into existence. With my brain!"

I shook his hand and he hugged me—a strange-smelling bear. I said good-bye and walked off into the night.

A few blocks away I could have sworn I heard him call out: "Remember! Prayer!" But I couldn't be sure. I like to think he did.

Along my walk I passed a couple sitting on the steps of a church kissing in the blue light of a spring night in Paris. I laid the brush at their feet, took out a pen, and wrote—or should I say, painted—in the small notebook I always carried with me two words: *Pray always.*

Brother Lawrence, the Re-Brainer, I have painted this book for you.

May God keep you safe.

Acknowledgements

I am deeply indebted to all the folks at Loyola Press for their warmth, kindness, enthusiasm, and support, including Terry Locke, Paul Campbell, Tom McGrath, Joellyn Cicciarelli, Andrew Yankech, Becca Russo, Judine O'Shea, and Yvonne Micheletti. What a dedicated team of creative professionals! I am also especially indebted to Joe Durepos, friend and mentor, for believing in this project and rescuing it from obscurity; and to Vinita Wright for her excellent editorial work and thoughtfulness.

Special thanks to Maura Zagrans, Mitch Horowitz, Anthony Destefano, James Martin, Deepak Chopra, Mickey Singer, Eric Hafker, Michael Stephenson, Lindsay Olson, J. Ivy, Will Romano, Marty Regine, Carie Freimuth, and Steve Cobb for their generosity, friendship, and inspiration.

I also want to thank my mom, Roseanne Jansen, and my sisters Mary, Annie, Julie, and Suzie as well as Fran, JoJo, Lenny, Carie, Teresa, Rob, Tina, Vicky, Joey, and Lucy, for all their love over the years.

Finally, I want to thank my wife, Grace, and my sons, Eddie and Charlie, for being mirrors that shine the light of God on me.

About the Author

Gary Jansen is senior editor of religion and spirituality at the Crown Publishing Group at Penguin Random House. He is the author of *The Rosary: A Journey to the Beloved* and the bestselling memoir, *Holy Ghosts*. A popular lecturer and commentator, Jansen has appeared on A&E, the Sundance Channel, the Travel Channel, Coast to Coast AM, CNN.com and NPR. His writing has been featured in the *Huffington Post*, *Religion Dispatches*, and *USA Today*.

Also Available

An Ignatian Book of Days
$12.95 | 4145-1 | PB

A Simple, Life-Changing Prayer
$9.95 | 3535-1 | PB

God Finds Us
$9.95 | 3827-7 | PB

Reimagining the Ignatian Examen
$9.95 | 4244-1 | PB